G000150691

The Confetti Culture Playbook

How to boost your team's contribution and impact

James Ferguson

DEDICATION

This book is dedicated to my smart, supportive, and loving
wife Caiti, and my two beautiful girls Grey and Izzy.

CONTENTS

ACKNOWLEDGMENTS

I would like to thank my incredibly supportive stepmom, Susan, and my loving wife, Caiti, who helped ensure I put out the best possible book I could. I want to thank my dad, Jay, and my mom, Christy, for their continued love and support. I am proud to be more like you both every day, and this book is a product of your mentorship. As well as my stepdad, Patrick, who helped guide and grow my business to what it is today. Lastly, I would like to thank the many people I have had the privilege to work with who inspired me to write this book and put *Family First.*

PREFACE

What if I told you that everything you needed to know about leadership and company culture was taught to you before the age of 6? What if I told you that you were conditioned at that young age to expect a certain level of structure, encouragement, involvement, appreciation, and care? As crazy as it sounds, it's true. Regardless of your socioeconomic status, race, color or creed, we are all conditioned at an elementary age to expect and need the same things. Yet, as wonderful and tragic as it sounds, at that young age we were unable to retain or appreciate the valuable information that then structured our lives. "Why is that," you might ask? It is simply because before the age of 6, the part of the brain that is crucial for memory formation is not fully developed. Therefore, our brains are only capable of storing peak moments and unconscious emotional memory. These two factors remove any opportunity to recollect the cultural structure and fundamental foundation our parents and teachers built. We forget like a distant memory how it shaped our lives, leaving us unfulfilled as we grow older and exit the schooling system. We then begin searching for employers and cultures that can fill the void, but nothing lives up to the hype. As professionals this leads us to jump from job to job in hopes for clarity and contentment. As leaders we begin searching for answers by reading books, listening to podcasts, and attending seminars in a continued effort to find answers to our questions. We do this all out of necessity to fill the void for ourselves and our teams. None of which seems to truly fulfill our craving and hunger, and so we remain unsatisfied. Sound familiar?

If this is your current reality, which I am almost certain it is, I can tell you now with great confidence I have the answers you've been searching for. I, too, have been on both sides of this scenario starting my career searching for a place to call home while, as a leader, exploring and learning how to create one. Like you, I have read book after book in hopes for answers, only getting a page or less of value out of 150. Like you I have attended seminars and retreats hoping for a roadmap, but leaving only energized and empty handed. So my search continued, collecting nuggets of information from each book and experience like pieces to a puzzle in hopes they will all come together providing the bigger picture we are all in search of. Little did I know that the missing pieces would be found in such a familiar place.

Power of Parenting

Let's start with your parents. At an infant age your parents encouraged and cared for you like none other, developing an unbreakable bond between you. Regardless of your personal upbringing whether traditional or not, that encouragement and care you received was created to build you up and promote specific behaviors for you to continue, even through the process of failure.

For example, as a baby when you became more mobile your parents began putting you on your back and encouraged and praised you as you attempted or succeeded in rolling over. Once you mastered that, they did the same things for crawling, and then walking. Whether it was learning letters, colors, using a fork, or teaching your daughter how to dunk on a Little Tikes easy score hoop like I am currently, the process remains the same. Whatever the new skill might be, they rewarded the behaviors they wanted to see more of by encouraging and praising you along the way. This concept psychologically led us into needing and seeking encouragement, approval, and praise as a motivator through the process of learning through failure. That's because there is no mastery without failure and the way through is encouragement. Can we cope without it? Of course we can, but the results are significantly better if it's there and it's consistent.

This concept remains true in business and in leadership as well. In order for a manager to lead and motivate her team she needs to encourage and praise the behaviors she wants to see. She needs to constantly be on the lookout for those positive behaviors and reinforce them through recognition and reward. But don't mistake rewards as only gifts. Remember, as children we are programmed to need and receive encouragement. Whether it is verbally with simple words like good job, visually by clapping, or physically with a pat on the back, they all serve as reward and encouragement. So don't over complicate it. This encouragement must happen every single day throughout the day like your parents did for you, and by the end of this book, like me, you will start throwing confetti in along the way, but we will get into that later.

Similar to parenting, as leaders we need to engage, enable, and empower our teams to make decisions and take actions they believe are the best choice in the moment. We need to encourage and guide them so that they feel supported through their decision making. That way they know and feel that you have their back, regardless of the outcome. If you encourage and incentivize your team by leading as your parents would, you will see significantly better results.

If you haven't figured it out yet, our parents are the familiar persons I was referring to earlier. Sometimes we work so hard to avoid being like them that we forget to be grateful for all they have taught us. This all clicked for me when I became a parent. Once my first daughter was born I quickly learned how to recognize and reward her to grow and improve. Being a parent is being a leader. It was that simple, yet it wasn't enough. A great leader with no structure is no leader at all. I found the answer to that in a familiar place as well. While improving a previous employer's company culture by building a sustainable framework it dawned on me. We were creating anticipation for our new employee driven initiatives by putting up posters in our back-of-house hallway when the HR manager said to me, this place is starting to look like a school. Right there and then I had an epiphany!

The Fun-damentals

Let's take a second to think back to your elementary school days. Take a moment to remember and reminisce the best parts of 1st to 5th grade. Now I want you to think of one word to describe your experience. As I reminisce, the word that comes to mind for me is Fun! Why is that? Because the people that developed the curriculum and calendar events for you at that age knew you needed fun, as it was a FUNdamental part of learning.

Next, I want you to think about some of the activities you remember from school at that age. For me I think of field trips, field day, holiday parties, gold stars, book fairs, cafeteria calendars, recess, and so much more. I bet thinking back to those simpler times puts a big smile on your face as it does mine. What's more interesting about that list and other nostalgic activities unmentioned is the correlation to leadership and company culture. Don't believe me? Let me explain.

If you were to research the areas of most importance to the average employee when seeking a new opportunity, it would be similar to the following:

- Clear expectations
- Resources needed to do the job
- Genuine Encouragement & Appreciation
- Ownership Opportunity
- Road map for achieving goals
- Recognition & Reward
- Growth Opportunity
- Performance feedback & coaching

- Communication
- Accountability
- Structure

Now take a moment to think back. As a 3rd grader did your teachers provide most of those for you? Mine sure did, as I am sure yours did too. What I am getting at is that each item on this list above directly correlates on a higher level to an activity from your elementary school days. As silly as it may sound it's true. That's because at an elementary age we are conditioned to expect and need the same things we do now, yet we ignore this truth by spending our entire childhood wishing we were grown up and more mature than we are. We start avoiding and fighting against anything that may resemble our childish ways, therefore suppressing the memories and the very principles that built our fun-damental foundation. Not until years later do we reminisce about our childhood days and all the fun we had. By then it's become too late to see the structure they provided. At that point we have compartmentalized our life in a way that those details don't stand out in our memory, avoiding any attempt to see the obvious truth that's been under our nose the entire time.

The point is this: the culture structure created around us as kids can and should be used on a higher level as adults. That day, walking back-of-house areas, I realized it was becoming more and more school-like around the building. While my instincts told me to avoid it at all costs, it became very clear we shouldn't fight it but instead embrace it. That's when things changed for the better and we slowly saw measurable progress we hadn't seen before.

Let me be clear. Just because the general cultural structure designed in elementary school can translate on a higher level into the workplace, that doesn't mean it's all that's needed when building a framework for a strong company culture. There are still multiple areas beyond that, which I've learned over the years is needed in order to truly have success in building a sustainable strong culture. I came to realize that over time as my team and I designed the framework mapped out in this book. I also learned that history repeating itself isn't always a bad thing, especially when you're building it better.

Nevertheless, what ultimately helped me see the big picture on how to build a successful and sustainable culture was not in a book, a podcast, or a seminar. The missing pieces to the puzzle were under my nose the entire time. My parents and teachers taught me everything I needed to know. When realized, it provided me the necessary tools and insight to build something truly special. Which is why I am compelled to now share it with you.

INTRODUCTION

After years of experience in effectively leading and managing hotel operations, I decided to redirect my leadership path. Through working alongside multiple ownership groups, operating flagged and independent properties, at limited and full-service levels I developed an ability to cultivate positive relationships and build successful teams across the hospitality spectrum.

My experiences helped me realize that in our industry we are taught to focus on guests and the all mighty dollar, not the people working hard to earn it for us. That's when I decided to start my own business to change the narrative, vowing to be the change I wanted to see in the industry by challenging the status quo. Now, I share my passion and experience with hospitality management teams to create a personalized and measurable framework designed to improve their financial position by realigning their priorities and putting employees *first*.

By giving top priority to the interests of your employees,

they will then give top priority to your guests, which will deliver top priority results to your owners. As you reap the rewards of this framework, you will increase employee retention through recognition and reward, allowing you to save on recruitment costs, while boosting contributions and impact.

Employee turnover in the hospitality industry is an escalating and urgent concern. Our industry alone experiences an employee turnover rate of roughly 73% which is exponentially higher than the annual average which typically sits at around 11%. This eye-opening statistic not only impacts your operations efficiency and guest experience, but also the financial stability and growth of your business.

In our customer-centric and guest facing industry, having employees constantly coming and going like a revolving door can make it difficult to meet or exceed guests' expectations. Let alone build loyalty to your business and brand. Not to mention the costly financial implications of constantly finding, hiring, and training new employees. While a certain degree of employee attrition is expected, there are things you can do to minimize it. In order to first understand how to keep employees around, you must first understand why they are leaving.

In this book, I outline a series of purpose driven employee initiatives that are designed around and expand beyond the 7 biggest causes of employee turnover in the hospitality industry. Those seven leading causes are as follows:

- Unclear Job Expectations

- Disconnect with Managers
- Toxic work Environment
- Inefficient Communication
- Lack of Flexibility
- Minimal Growth Opportunity
- Lack of Recognition & Reward

While these seven strong reasons to leave are hard to argue, they don't stand a chance against the initiatives I provide ahead. Allow me to guide you through the process of building a better culture by infusing what I know and what we've learned from both our parents and teachers and applying it to your daily operation. I hope you are as excited as I am to start this journey together. Let's start the transformation process, or as I like to say...*Let's get it!*

1 SET EXPECTATIONS

Have you ever been reprimanded for not meeting expectations, but were never formally informed or trained to know that in the first place? Have you ever worked somewhere that you only saw your manager when something went wrong? Worse yet, have you, yourself, reprimanded an employee for not meeting expectations that you never personally vocalized or reviewed? Instead of holding yourself accountable for your team's results, you put the burden of training and equipping a new employee on their underperforming and uninterested coworker. Unfortunately, I have seen all sides of this unfold time and time again, and like you, I have been a victim on far too many occasions over the years to unvocalized expectations. Using reprimand to set your expectations or faulting your employee for lack of initiative and adaptability when you never gave them a fair chance, is a guaranteed way to send people packing. As the leader of a department or business, it is your job to proactively provide expectations and consistently coach for improvement. That means all the time and on-going. Expectations aren't a one and done thing, and accountability starts with you.

In this chapter I will be providing you with a clear road map for leadership success by showing you how to set expectations. I will give you insights required to be proactive and not reactive, making sure you understand the value in providing your team with the time, tools, and training necessary to achieve those set expectations, as well as ways to monitor, measure, and motivate progress toward meeting them. It's time to be better, so lets be better together!

Leadership

Everything rises and falls on leadership. Therefore, if you aren't seeing the results and behaviors you expect from your team that's on you. Like I previously mentioned, leadership is similar to parenting, which means you need to coach, recognize, and reward the behaviors you want to see. It's not about fancy titles, fear, or power. It's about investing in people. It's a conscious decision, and a daily commitment you make. It's not about managing people; it's about inspiring them.

Great leaders build successful teams by utilizing and valuing the strengths of each individual within the group. They provide a clear vision, energized by collectively set standards, which will inspire their team to achieve their true potential. They continually cultivate positive relationships through equipping and mentoring that ensures their team feels both valued and appreciated, all while remaining approachable and leading with a constructive and motivational approach. I know it seems like a lot to juggle - it is. By following this formula you too can be a great leader. But like anything worthwhile it takes work. You have to live it. It takes commitment and it takes discipline. I will elaborate on this further in the coming chapters, but as mentioned, it starts with providing a clear vision and set of expectations.

When leading a team, setting expectations isn't just about a list on a paper, or the power behind it. It's about communicating it through action. This means as a leader your expectations need to be upheld by you, before anyone will do the same. Expectations aren't just about holding your team accountable, it's more importantly about holding yourself accountable. Unfortunately, many people as they climb the ladder and get promoted become entitled and act like they have arrived. They adopt the motto to, *do as I say, not as I do,* which is a terrible way to lead. You need to walk the talk and lead by example, otherwise everyone will form their own habits and behaviors. Before you know it, your culture will become the Wild West, because if you're not following the rules, why should they? Don't make those same mistakes. Take notes, and take action to build a better tomorrow today.

Whether it's an annual theme, your company mission statement, your core values, your standard operating procedures, or your personal leadership expectations, the same rules apply for all. You don't just make them and move on. You dont post them somewhere and magically people live them out. They take work. Through continued education, encouragement, training and development they can evolve into a purpose driven way of life, but you need to nurture your people like you would nurture a child. This doesn't mean you should treat your employees like children, although some may act like it. It simply means you need to lead like a parent, not like a person in power.

Proactive vs Reactive

As a new parent in 2019, I quickly developed the instincts to protect my own when Grey, my first daughter, was born. In preparation for her arrival, I wrote her a letter which I feel applies to this and so I wanted to share it with you. It reads:

Dear Grey,

Most parents spend their lives giving their kids everything they never had and attempting to protect them from this cold cruel world. But what we forget is all the things we went through in our lives helped shape who we have become. So as I get ready to bring you into this world I will shift my thinking from protect to prepare. Because, I can't protect you from everything. But I can prepare you, and so I will.

Love,

Dada

The reason I share this letter with you is this; as a parent I realized I can't protect my daughters from everything. The same applies to leadership. You can't control or protect your team from all the different scenarios that will come their way. What you can control though is how well you prepare them to handle it. This is what being proactive looks like: identifying and preventing potential problems by creating structure and solutions through preparation. Not by being a problem identifier, but rather a problem solver, in advance. It's controlling the narrative and the outcomes, rather than responding after it's too late.

I reported to a manager once that was very reactive. At that time my colleagues said we complimented each other well because I was all the things he was not and it balanced things out around the property. I later learned there was a lot more that he lacked, than what he brought to the table. I had to pick up a lot of his slack, but that's a tale for another time.

Nevertheless, he used to always tell me he was there to protect me. Protect me from failure, humiliation, and judgement by my peers and even corporate. He put me under his wing, made me believe he was my protector, and that I was safe to grow under him. Unfortunately, it took me far too long to realize he was only protecting himself by sheltering me from growing by taking credit for my efforts for his benefit. The way he would "protect me" from unfavorable outcomes was that if he noticed something not going as he expected, he would swoop in the eleventh hour and solve things himself. He never made any effort to prepare me in advance, coach me, or allow me to deliver it myself.

One year we had our CEO hosting a tree lighting Christmas party at our hotel, so I needed to facilitate the decorating of the property to ensure it was a good representation of, not only me in my new role, but the CEO and the company. My boss expressed the importance of us hosting the event, but never provided expectations or insights on how to deliver on his or corporate expectations. He simply scheduled a walk-through a few days prior to the event. I began preparing my plan, using our budget to cost things out, and getting the needed team members involved to execute.

We were right on schedule and I was prepared to answer any timeline questions he had for our walk. On the day of the walk he made it clear we had failed. Not enough this, too little that. He said, "I told you the importance of this event, did you seriously think this was acceptable? You're not even close to ready and it's 3 days away." I was embarrassed, frustrated, and ill prepared for what transpired, but that was how he handled himself regularly. His management style was a reactive one, never proactive. He then spent a shit ton of money we didn't have on decor, and labor hours we didn't need, to fix something he set up to fail while looking like the hero from the outside looking in. In his eyes, he may have protected me from the CEO I saw maybe 4 times a year. But he humiliated me in front of everyone on my team and undermined weeks of hard work done by so many people, in true Extreme Makeover fashion. The moral of the story is this; Protection can be problematic, but preparation is proactive. Being proactive is being ready so you never have to get ready. I adapted and learned from him and this experience as I hope you will. Nothing good came from his reactive style, except that I learned from his many mistakes and ensured I never did the same.

Learn from everyone. Not just the good stuff, but the bad stuff too. Every decision made, whether yours or someone else's, has a lesson attached to it. Pay close attention and build your leadership style not just on all the things you want to be, but also on all the things you don't. Learn from the best and worst of people, adopting habits accordingly.

Lasty, I want to share a proactive tool that Ive used to counteract a major demotivator in the traditional performance improvement plan, or PIP. These plans typically are implemented as a last resort prior to termination to either coach someone up or out of the organization. It then puts all the accountability on the manager to consistently measure and monitor progress when it's already too late. That's why I've started using the 5Ps proactive plan. What this plan does is help you predict, plan, participate, prevent, and perform better on a continual basis with your team. No one should be getting put on a PIP, because if they are, you the manager, are just as much to blame. So get ahead of it. Hold yourself accountable to your team members' progress by using this tool to continually improve monthly.

Set Clear Expectations

Providing clear expectations is a key to your individual and team success. As clearly spelled out in the story about my old boss, by not setting clear expectations up front you instead set your team up for failure. That's why it's important to set them early and often.

Let me ask you this, have you ever written down your leadership expectations? If not, I highly recommend it. Here's why. If you haven't put them on paper yet it means one of two things. Either they aren't truly defined, or it means you personally don't want to be held accountable to them. But if you don't even know what they are, and aren't willing to live up to them, how do you expect your team to?

Now you might be asking yourself where do I begin, what should I include? Ultimately, you will need to figure out and define yours on your own. In order to monitor and motivate your team to exceed expectations you need to have them set to see if they are measuring up.

The best way to start formulating your expectations is starting with your highest priority. In my roles managing hotels, contrary to popular belief, I start with who I serve, which is my employees. They are the foundation of our success, which I hope by the end of this book you adopt this same mindset. My next priority would be who our employees serve, which is our guests. By making our employees our first priority, they will in turn put our guest as their first priority.

For hoteliers reading this, in our industry we are taught to focus on guests and the all mighty dollar, not the people working hard to earn it for us. See, what we fail to remember is who is responsible for creating the memorable moments that lead to exceeded expectations. It's your employees. They have a direct link to our guests and the quality of product and service they receive, yet the status quo in our industry is that guests pay the bills. It's time we realign our priorities as an industry. That's why it has become my mission to build a culture of valued employees who are engaged, enabled, and empowered to be at their best and deliver their best daily. Which then builds guest loyalty to the business and the brand. Talk about clear expectations. Take it from someone who has implemented and observed first-hand the positive impact and results achieved by this shift.

From there my list of expectations supports the top two priorities. Including things like attitude, empowerment, responsibility, support, quality of life, consistency, professionalism, attention to detail, etc. Once you find your top 2 or 3 priorities, the remainder of your expectations are in support of delivering on them.

Hopefully, by providing you this insight it will allow you to easily formulate your own. This list does not have to be perfect and will change over time so just start by putting words on paper.

Once your expectations have been set, it's time to deliver them. This doesn't mean in a scary email or memo by the time clock saying, "do this or else." They should be communicated in a well thought out meeting delivered in an empathetic and engaging way. Whether it's your first week on the job or you are years in, if you haven't provided clear expectations to your team it's time to do so. Providing expectations delivers vision, purpose, and accountability. Not just for your team but also for you. So when you have this meeting make sure you ask for their commitment to deliver, as well as their support to ensure you deliver as well. This collective commitment will go a long way in the eyes of your team and show them the power of an all-in attitude.

Time, Tools, and Training

I remember first hearing the phrase time, tools, and training from the Assistant General Manager of a hotel I worked at in Center City Philadelphia. It was my first experience with a manager who understood the value of his people, and returning his knowledge back into the world to better others. He was an inspiring guy and I definitely adopted some of his habits as I shaped my own leadership style early in my career. He taught me that providing time, tools, and training meant investing in your team. Investing your time in people through conversation, encouragement, motivation, and support. Investing money into the tools necessary to deliver basic job functions. As well as investing in equipping your employees through on-going training. Remembering that even professional athletes need training to stay on point and do so regularly. That continued education is a key to continued growth, so don't underestimate the value of ongoing training; it's essential to your team's success.

Leadership is about serving your people, not the other way around. By investing in them in these three ways your team will improve exponentially. It will allow them the opportunity to provide the best quality of product or service possible. On the other hand, if you were to remove one or more of these 3 investments from the equation you are bound to fail overtime. Expectations are for you just as much as your team to live up to, thus it's crucial you develop a plan that works for you to ensure consistency.

For me, consistency was created through scheduling. Scheduling through my work calendar on my computer and phone with alerts and notifications to keep me on point. As well as an at a glance accountability calendar which I separately created to keep me intentionally planning ahead. These two scheduling systems both micro and macro, remind me to set time aside for my people both individually and as a team. For example, to have a scheduled inventory monthly to keep me up to date on tools needed to do the job, as well as have scheduled training sessions throughout the month. They keep me planning, prepared, and proactive in delivering the needed time, tools, and training to my team. Find what works best for you to stay consistent, and start investing in those 3 areas today.

Monitor, Measure, and Motivate!

In order to monitor and motivate your team to exceed expectations you need to have them set, in order to understand how they are measuring up. Now that your expectations have been written down and set, you need to build your SOPs, training, and incentives around delivering and exceeding them.

Since my top expectation is that employees come first in all that we do, I needed to figure out measurable ways to increase employee retention through reward and recognition. By creating this measurable framework, it would then allow us to save on recruitment, training, and boost contributions and impact. For this reason, my team and I at the time worked hard to discover the best ways to deliver on the needs of our people. Through this process, I began to recognize the similarities between the structure we were building, and the structure we once had as kids in school. They were ways to deliver better communication, ownership, growth opportunity, community, recognition, and reward. By improving in these areas and having our employees at the forefront of all our decision making, it became clear that this change would contagiously impact our guest experience in a positive way.

Same rules applied for our second priority. We needed to develop a framework that was built to exceed expectations for our guests, so we developed training plans that taught, encouraged, and rewarded the behaviors we wanted to see from our people, just like a parent would. This continued on for every expectation I had. I created roadmaps to achieve our goals. Whether it be empowerment, communication, attitude, or attention to detail, there were plans in place for nurturing those behaviors. The purpose was to ensure my team's understanding, implementation, and ongoing improvement in achieving operational excellence. Again, this may sound like a lot to manage, but the more you have planned out and prepped the easier it is to sustain and build off of. Which you, too, will learn through your own journey.

In the same ways I built around my expectations a measurable way to monitor and motivate my team, it's now time you do the same. Line by line developing ways to support each commitment and then holding everyone accountable along the way. When you are consistent with your commitments, and consistent with support and development, it keeps everyone on track and working towards a common goal. It also removes the negative connotation when holding people accountable because if people are off track, it's due to their own choosing, and they'll know the conversation is coming. It will also be seen as just another teaching moment, to grow and be better together.

2 DAILY HUDDLE

Everyone knows Murphy's Law. Everything that can go wrong will go wrong. Unfortunately, that's exactly what I walked into at the start of a new role a few years back. It didn't take me but a few hours into my first shift to realize that my new team had an every man for himself mentality. They were stuck in their Wild West ways, driven by fear into a great divide. Any chance they got they would throw each other under the bus, never taking ownership, and only coming together when shit hit the fan or when forced to by fear. Does that sound like your organization? God, I hope not. Needless to say, if this sounds like your team dynamic you have your work cut out for you as did I, not just with the line level employees, but with senior leadership as well. We needed a total overhaul, and it wasn't going to get fixed overnight, but I was up for the challenge. In the coming pages, I will be providing you the first piece of the puzzle that helped me transform my new team, giving you insight into the benefits of implementing this daily practice in case you too are facing a similar challenge. It all started with a huddle.

What I refer to as Huddle, may be better known as a stand-up meeting. The reason I call it a huddle is because in the similar way a sports team huddles before a play, I use it as a time to positively gather together to strategize, motivate, and celebrate together before each day. Something I learned quickly was desperately needed with my new team. Huddle done twice a day can improve communication, collaboration, cohesiveness, and celebration, if consistent. It provides a daily opportunity to inspire my team, much like a coach does at half time, which I don't take lightly.

In the hotel industry, a typical standup meeting is when managers tell other managers what they got on their plate for the day so that everyone's aware of the day's events. In order for this time to connect to truly have a measurable impact we would need to be a little more intentional than conventional.

I remember as I was getting to know that team, meeting one-on-one with employees, I had mentioned countless times the idea of implementing huddle as a resolution to some of their communicated issues. Each time I mentioned it, I was met with push back and a response like, "we tried that it doesn't work here." Little did they know, the reason it had not worked in the past was due to the fact that no one was leading the conversation, or inspiring the change needed in order to be better together. I needed to design this meeting in a way that would improve communication, collaboration, cohesiveness, and celebration.

Communication

Communication is a growth opportunity for every business on the planet, so don't panic if that's brought up in one of your employee surveys. There are plenty of ways to improve it and, lucky for you, I will be providing plenty of solutions in this book.

One of the biggest problems with communication is the illusion that it takes place. My new team had expressed to me early and often through our meetings, that they had standup meetings in the past, communicating daily, and it didn't resolve their issues. Many times, in communicating we do not listen with the intent to understand but rather to respond or in this case attack. This team was so divided that the only time people communicated was behind each other's back or in attack mode when things fell apart. This would happen far too often, unfortunately. This meant there was a lot of unnecessary built-up frustration between one another. It was important that I addressed it and became a change agent.

That's why I reintroduced the morning standup, with a new name, a new time, and a new structure. The time shifted from 9am to 10am. It was no longer just for managers to attend. Line level employees were invited and encouraged to join, allowing them to gain exposure, learn operations, and build relationships beyond their department. The rebranding and reformatting of this morning meeting was to remove the negative connotation currently attached to it, to build team unity by positively coming together, as well as a shift in start time to provide an additional hour of time to assess the day. This allowed those who maybe started their day at 9am to have some time to assess where the needs were, and be able to communicate it to the rest of the team so we could support daily instead of stay separate.

One of the ways I reformatted our daily huddle was by leading the conversation with intention, setting my expectations for the day, the week, or both. They didn't have that prior. Stand ups prior consisted of going around the room, cutting the tension with a knife, and running back to their desks. The GM never attended the huddle either, which was also part of the problem. With no one leading by example or towards a common goal and vision, it was no wonder it hadn't worked in the past. Attendance was low and rather unproductive. I attended daily and led the conversation, using my time to articulate purpose and communicate daily. I kept everyone up to date on current events, on our financial well being, and any adjustments we needed to commit to in order to be better together.

An example of how I used this platform to articulate purpose and motivate my team like a coach, is by introducing a Quote of the Week to be discussed as a group for individual and collective growth. Just like the rest of you I need inspiration and motivation too. So at the beginning of each week I would write down the quote of the week on the white board on my office door in order to share it with the group. But it wasn't just about reading the quote aloud, it was more about inspiring action. Quotes are only words unless we live by them. For example, if the quote of the week was:

"You'll never change your life until you change

something you do daily. The secret to your success is found in your daily routine."

I would read it aloud and ask them what they thought it meant. In this case I would ask them if they believed they were personally or collectively exceeding expectations. I would then encourage them to look at what they do daily, and adjust to ensure each habit is guiding them in the right direction to achieve their leadership and departmental goals. I also explain how huddle is an example of a daily habit that will be a secret to our success. I then would circle back throughout the week to learn more about how the team was applying it's principles.

I do this at the start of every week, providing 52 quotes annually to motivate and mold our people to be better together one week at a time. Even more important to this specific group, was the sharing of positive stories, the celebration of personal and team wins, and the collective commitments made daily to one another.

Collaboration

Collaboration was an important element to introduce into our daily dynamic. As mentioned, the team was so divided so it was important we not only shared our departmental struggles verbally but also physically, by collectively committing to support one another through completion. We also had a divide between the AM team and the PM team, which led me to introduce a second huddle at 5pm allowing a time daily for both shifts to connect, communicate, and collaborate. Again, teaching the team to be better together.

For example, if the food & beverage department had a houseman call out on the events team, and we had an hour to flip the event space for a new event this would be communicated in huddle, and once huddle concluded, all those who attended would go help support and set the room. In the past, the manager in food and beverage would be "left on an island" to do it all herself, and then without empathy or support, be harassed later by the sales team for not delivering a good product to the client. Notice the difference?

What I needed to do was teach the team through consistent collaboration, that everyone has a hand in whether we fail or succeed. That many of the challenges we face could be resolved and avoided if we simply worked with each other instead of against one another. I taught daily that the only thing divided should be our task lists, which will in turn multiply our collective success. This concept took time and patience from everyone involved to develop. Ultimately, overtime helping us rebuild our broken relationships and team unity. It provided understanding and inspired new ideas. It created shared fate. Yet it wasn't enough. We needed additional reinforcement that would come through strategic planning and well thought out intentional activities.

Cohesiveness

The way to build a better team is through ongoing strategic planning, and through well thought out, intentional activities that promote togetherness, collaboration, collective responsibility and team unity. How do you do that you ask? By sprinkling in periodic team building activities like confetti into our daily huddles.

Most people hate team building, because it makes them uncomfortable. I do it anyway as it is a vital tool in developing cohesiveness. To be excellent, we needed to be comfortable with the uncomfortable. Interesting enough, whether people are committed to the process of a team building exercise or not, it doesn't really matter. Subconsciously, the laughter and fun involved in it helps them learn what I am looking to teach. See fun is a fun-demetnal part of learning. It creates a positive memory with the group. And even if they talk shit afterward, just like a funny commercial, they're still talking about it. So you still win. Everyone still learns and over time this makes a substantial difference.

There are plenty of books out there about team building with thousands of ideas that teach a series of topics, which you should strategically schedule based on the teams needs at the time. Whether it's holiday inspired, like a halloween mummy wrapping contest using toilet paper; or a human knot activity where it promotes communication; or even something as simple as grabbing 2 tissue boxes and seeing who can empty their box first one tissue at a time, the options are endless. These activities should be sprinkled in randomly to not only break up the monotony, but also continue to create creative positive interaction between your divided team.

I remember when Kobe Bryant passed away, it shocked the world and taught us all to be grateful. For huddle the next day, I had my team write down on a piece of paper what they were most grateful for, share it with the group, and then we collectively shot it into a trash can yelling KOBE! It was spontaneous, relevant, and impactful.

Don't waste time racking your brain for ideas for hours on end. Use tools and resources readily available to you to keep things simple. As I've said, being proactive and planning things out always adds greater value and impact. But sometimes, like in the above example, it's good to throw a spontaneous exercise in to remind everyone to be grateful. But nothing quite impacts a team like recognition and reward.

Celebration

The easiest way to increase employee retention is through reward and recognition. These simple celebrations, orchestrated during daily huddle and beyond, will greatly boost contributions and impact, yet so few managers and organizations follow through on it consistently.

Through celebration, you are encouraging the behaviors you want to continue to see. Confetti has become a tool that represents the transforming power of recognition and reward in a company culture. Confetti has the power to immediately transform the energy in any room. By using confetti in celebration, you immediately shift the energy in the room from doom and gloom, to KABOOM! Energy is contagious. The energy you produce is vital as a leader. It sets the tone. So by adding a positive energy element like confetti to every recognition and celebration, it contagiously spreads that energy well beyond huddle into the rest of the organization, from the heart of the house to the front of the house. Needless to say confetti has sort of become my trademark. It's a powerful and positive tool that like a special occasion brings people together. If not, as it's thrown in the air, it will at least bring people together as you clean it up. I also like to think of confetti as an element of accountability for continued recognition because if you don't see it around the building you'll know people aren't being recognized.

Confetti is harder to clean up than you think. Even after your team cleans it up, you will still find confetti that stuck around long after it's thrown. In back of house areas I don't require it to be picked up immediately. In fact, we embrace and encourage it on the floor, reason being is it shows all that walk by it or through it that someone or something was celebrated, recognized, and rewarded. This promotes others to do the same for one another, as well as creates excitement and anticipation as they, too, strive to be confettied for their accomplishments.

You may be asking yourself when should confetti be used during huddle and I'd say any time, but below are a few of the crucial celebrations you should stay on top of for your people and be prepared to celebrate with confetti.

- Birthdays
- Anniversaries
- Personal accomplishments
- Promotions
- New hires
- 5 star reviews
- Employee of the Month
- Achieving Departmental Profit goals

Sometimes these celebrations are facilitated by just me, and other times it's a group effort. The point is they energize and inspire your team to celebrate themselves, each other, and do it often. Confetti always leads to smiles and claps, it's a proven side effect. So this becomes a valuable and vital tool to use with a team that is divided and needs realignment.

Celebrations must be consistent and happen daily when applicable. But don't read about it, be about it. Be the change you want to see by consistently recognizing your people and cascading confetti any chance you get.

3 GENUINE APPRECIATION

Have you ever felt unheard, unnoticed, underpaid, and undervalued? If that's your current situation it's most likely due to the fact that your manager or organization does not invest time or energy into employee appreciation. If they do, it's misguided, inconsistent, and ingenuine. Most people identify appreciation as the single most important action a leader can take to improve effort levels and produce better results. Oftentimes managers are so focused on themselves that they fail to find out the needs of those they lead, leaving the opportunity to improve turnover, engagement, contribution and impact to mere chance.

As I've mentioned, we are all conditioned at an infant age to need and seek encouragement, approval, and praise as a motivator. Appreciation is our greatest emotional need. It's recognizing someone's worth and potential and expressing your belief in them. Therefore, if an employee isn't receiving it where they are now, they will surely make plans to go somewhere that will. The issue I find in most hotels is that recognition and reward is not given equally to all levels of the organization, if at all. Line level employees tend to have significantly less recognition and reward than managers and above. This is something that immediately needs to change.

Employees are our greatest asset and it's time we all start acting like it. I am embarrassed to remind you that the turnover rate in the hospitality industry is exponentially higher than any other industry in the world. This is due to the fact that the majority of hotel owners value guests over employees. It is ingrained in our brains when entering the industry that our focus and highest priority is on our guests. While I know I have an uphill battle ahead to inspire change, a simple realignment of our focus, by putting employees first, can change everything for the better and have a profound positive effect on the guest experience. It's time to change the statistics and be the difference. As a result, you will see exponential increases in engagement and effort. And the influence you will have both in the short and longer term on your people and your profits will prove rapid and robust.

In this chapter about appreciation, I will be providing you with practical and sustainable employee appreciation initiatives that scale across your organization, ensuring every single person on your team feels valued and appreciated. Through consistent recognition and reward, your employees will undoubtedly do more to improve your business. Allow me to provide some insight on best practices and why recognition should start on the first day and flow consistently throughout the duration of a person's employment.

Recognition & Reward

You are going to hear me say the words recognize and reward a lot in this book. That's truly the difference between where you are and where you could be culturally. The repetitive nature of my writing is much like the way a teacher repeats things in class that will be on a future test. Repetition is the first principle of learning, so as you're reading, if you notice I'm repeating something often, you should probably take notes on whatever it is, as it is highly important to your future success. Don't worry, there's no formal test, although your culture can fail like you would a test if you're unprepared and inconsistent.

Recognition is not just about recognizing good work in the moment. While that is an important element, it is actually much deeper than that. We as leaders have a responsibility to develop strong and meaningful relationships with our people just like we do with our customers. If we don't first put that effort in internally, how do we expect our team to do it externally? You need to recognize who people are. Recognize their interests, their contributions, their effort, their progress, their potential, their value, and even their personality. You need to recognize their successes, their failures, their feelings, their attitude, energy, and their actions. Recognition goes well beyond a birthday celebration. Recognition is about expressing value through action. It's about building and strengthening relationships. It ensures each person on your team feels valued, cared for, listened to, and supported like a child does from their parents. From there, you will see dramatic improvement in engagement, effort, and efficiency throughout the operation all because you cared for and about your people. You have to recognize and care about every part of them, not just what they can do for you. Once you do that, you can utilize the strengths of each individual in the group to build a more successful team.

Reward, on the other hand, is about motivating, encouraging, and celebrating the behaviors you want to see with a gift for great work. Don't go on a witch hunt to find people making mistakes. Instead, intentionally spend time on the floor trying to find people doing good and reward them for it. When you do this you will notice your team's energy shift dramatically when you're around. They will seek your approval and appreciate your presence, rather than fear it. Remember, reward can be all sorts of things from high fives to lunch on you, so don't over complicate it. It's not about the dollar amount, it's about the gesture and the power behind it. The key is to continually look for and reward the good, and you will be amazed how much more of it you see.

In order for you to boost contribution and impact at your hotel, you will need to find ways to implement recognition and reward across the board, not just within your senior leadership circle. Make sure it filters all the way down the depth chart, otherwise the negative effects over time will force not only your line level employees out, but your managers, too. Lucky for you, I provide recognition efforts that can be applied at all levels of your operation that expand well beyond this chapter. So, keep your highlighters handy and let's start with the first day.

First Impression

First impression starts the moment you hire someone. So every step you take or don't take from there on will influence her belief and buy-in into the purpose and company culture. That's why it is important to value the first impression and create a memorable experience that sticks with her forever.

It's important to start this process immediately following the signing of their offer letter. Once they have signed, you should request a short bio on them and a photo to use to inform the current team about them prior to their arrival, allowing them to feel welcome and comfortable when they start their first day. Next, send an email creating familiarity by informing them where to park, where to enter, what to wear, and anything else you may feel important, as well as the name and photo of the team member who will be welcoming them at the door on their first day. That way you eliminate some of the unknowns and limit first day jitters for your valued new hire.

From there, it's important your new hire feels welcome and that you are prepared for their arrival. This means if they are a manager, you should prepare their computer and desk to be usable on day one, including a banner that says welcome to the family. And maybe even provide a small gift that represents your company and your appreciation for them choosing to join your team.

That first day, they should be scheduled to arrive at 9am and be greeted by a familiar face to welcome them outside the back door and provide them access to get in. Arriving at this time allows her to walk back-of-house areas and get the lay of the land, as well as be introduced to some new co-workers who already know her name and say, "hi" using it. This again, goes a long way in providing comfortability on a rather uncomfortable first day. Then, at 10am, bring them to your huddle where they are formally introduced to the team and showered with confetti, expressing excitement for their arrival. In huddle, the team members clap in celebration while expressing support, putting their mind at ease. After huddle, they are shown to their desk and see the welcome sign and gift that you had prepared for them. In that moment they realize they made a great decision by accepting our offer.

Next, they are provided with their email address, and allowed some time to settle in. The first message is from you, the GM, introducing yourself, your culture, and genuinely expressing your gratitude and excitement for her choosing your company. What should that email consist of? See below for an example of what I've sent in the past for you to use as a reference.

Hi [Insert Name],

Welcome to the [Insert Company] Family! We are ecstatic you accepted our offer, and we are eager to work with you. We are confident that someone with your talent and skills will be an amazing addition to our team. Your role is critical in fulfilling our mission and we hope you are excited for the opportunity!

The following information is designed to serve as an introduction and provide resources that will help you make a smooth transition into your new role.

First I want to introduce you to our purpose driven theme which is *Family First*. What *Family First* means to us is making our Employees our first priority who will in turn put our guest as their first priority, as our employees have a direct link to our guests and the quality of product and service they receive.

It is our mission to build a culture of valued employees, meaning you :), who are engaged, enabled, and empowered to be at their best and deliver their best daily which will build guest loyalty to the business and the brand.

It is very important to us that we deliver on that with you, so that you are empowered to invest in your people and our collective mission to build a *Family First* culture within your department. Please be open and honest through this transition process to ensure we do so. By doing this we believe you will have an opportunity to take this team to the next level, helping them be the best they've ever been.

As you begin this new adventure your first few days will be flexible allowing you the freedom to get to know the operation and your team as you see fit. We will also introduce you to your team, supporting managers, our executive team, as well as set some time aside for you and I to connect to discuss expectations.

We hope you are as excited as we are to have you start your first day. Our hope is that this introduction is helpful as you begin to get integrated. Enjoy your orientation and we look forward to your long, successful, and fulfilling career here at [Insert Company]!

Sincerely,

[Insert your Name]

Also, in her email she will see that at 1030am she has scheduled time to meet with a few fellow managers to better understand the operation, and ensure that she understands her underlying purpose and begins to appreciate her impact on the bigger picture.

Later that day, you link up with her for an off-site lunch bringing fellow team members along to continue the family first welcome and message. This will allow you some time to better get to know one another personally while keeping it relaxed and fun. After lunch, she will be provided the flexibility to do what she feels necessary to get better acclimated in her new role, and as the day winds down they will leave that first day feeling a sense of belonging, that their contributions matter. That's an inspiring way to start. The remainder of that first week will combine celebration with shadowing and counselling by an experienced manager, ensuring expectations are set, and confidence is built by equipping them to tackle their new role. You'll be providing an experience she will never forget, and will have staff looking to get involved to relive the experience.

Celebration of Service

Remembering and recognizing milestones is a crucial element to building a strong culture, but so often it is overlooked. Something as simple as recognizing a person's investment of time, energy, and effort in an organization goes a very long way in the longevity of an employees career with an organization. After all, we spend more of our waking hours at work than we do with the ones we love, so we should recognize that sacrifice and not take it lightly. Regardless of position or level of contribution everyone deserves a thank you for each and every year they invest. That's why I implement a Celebration of Service program everywhere I have the privilege to work.

The Celebration of Service employee initiative has 3 phases to it. The purpose behind it is to recognize employees' investment in serving our people and our customers. The first phase is an email recognizing their contributions over the last year that may read something like:

Dear [Insert Name]

Congratulations! Today marks your 1 year anniversary with the [insert company] Family. I wanted to personally reach out and congratulate you on reaching this significant milestone. Your loyalty and dedication to our clients and team alike have made a significant difference in the success of our businesses over the last year. We know that our growth and improvement is dependent on great people like you, and we just wanted to take a moment to say thank you and celebrate YOU!

Thank you for all you have done, and are continually doing to make this place great. As you reach this milestone and set new goals for the remainder of the year, we hope that you take time to reflect and take pride in knowing you are a vital member of our team. It is with great excitement we present you with this digital copy of your Celebration of Service certificate for 1 year of employment. We look forward to celebrating with you and presenting this in person on [Insert Date].

Again, thank you for your commitment and sacrifice and we look forward to a continued bright and successful future together!

Sincerely,

You

While this first draft seems rather impersonal in the generic verbiage above, it is simply acting as a guide for you to base yours off of. When you actually write your version of this email, you will want to customize it to fit the specific person it's for, mentioning years worked, accomplishments made, and excitement for their future possibilities.

The second phase is a Celebration of Service Brunch. The way this is orchestrated is you plan and host an event to celebrate all the people with anniversaries in a given month regardless of the years of service. For example, if it's May, and you have 10 people with anniversaries that month ranging from 1-5 years of service with the company, you invite them all to join you in celebration of your time together. At the event, you provide a hot meal to share together creating fellowship. The event would be structured to share stories, celebrate contributions, and recognize each employee personally.

The 3rd phase of this initiative is providing a framed certificate and gift, specific to the milestone each person is celebrating. This is a small genuine gesture to take home and be proud of for their time serving our guests and one another, and reminding them that we value them, their loyalty, and their commitment to bettering our business. These gifts can range from pins, to hats, to shirts, to jackets or whatever it is you feel represents your business and appreciation best. As they are recognized one by one, you allow them to say a few words if they choose and even snap a quick photo with the General Manager in remembrance of the moment. This process grows the appreciation in the room and creates a special moment that motivates them to stay for many years to come.

At the conclusion of this event you get a group photo taken where everyone holds up their gifts and smiles as confetti falls from the sky. An event like this hosted monthly, will significantly improve an employees feeling of appreciation and gratitude from its employer, but (like each area of opportunity I mention in this book) if you are not consistent in your delivery of such events it can create the very opposite effect. Stay disciplined and deliver the same care and kindness to everyone on your team each and every month of the year.

Monthly Meal

I want to start this section of the chapter off by making sure you know out the gate that treating your employees like crap can't be resolved by pizza parties. To be clear, treating employees like crap doesn't always mean you berate them. In fact, It can be much more subtle than that. For example, if you're not providing the tools to do the job you're treating your employees like crap. If you take credit and place blame you're treating your employees like crap. If you don't communicate expectations and reprimand them for your mistake, you're treating your employees like crap. If you have favorites and don't provide equal opportunity to all, then you are treating your employees like crap. You get the point I'm trying to get across. In order for a monthly meal to work as genuine appreciation, you have to be doing the basics as a leader first, then and only then providing an occasional lunch becomes an added bonus, reaffirming your team's belief that you care and genuinely appreciate them.

Similar to our elementary school days with cafeteria calendars and holiday inspired parties, I have found that implementing a monthly meal inspired by holidays really helps bring the team together. In hotels, there are many different departments all working towards a common goal but rarely do they require physical interaction. Most things are communicated through written or verbal communication throughout the day, so to provide a monthly opportunity for a hotel family to have cross departmental conversations in the break room and bond while filling their bellies for free, adds great value to your team. It builds relationships, creates unity, and breaks down barriers, while creating a positive memory to enjoy and look back on.

Remember to have fun with these meals. Using the holidays to inspire the food, games, and decorations involved. If it makes sense for your organization maybe even create a care committee of volunteers that focus on executing these meals and other employee driven events to ensure consistency and care.

To assist in getting your juices flowing on where to start with these meals, allow me to provide you with some inspiration from examples I've been part of in the past. In January we celebrate new beginnings. A great way to bring in the new year is to serve breakfast to your entire team working on the 1st. Not only is this a thank you to those who may have had to work all night on NYE, and still showed up committed the next day, but it's also just a positive way to introduce the new year and reaffirm your employees belief in your thinking and care for them.

Valentine's day falls in February and while everyone may not have someone to celebrate with romantically, it's important you are intentional in providing an opportunity for people on your team to come together and not spend it alone. A great food choice for this monthly meal is ordering heart shaped pizzas from your local pizzeria. Most pizza spots do it on that day and it provides a fun instagram moment for people to share, as well.

In March, we celebrate St. Patty's day by providing personal pints of Guinness to everyone that works that day. NOT! (Lol) But we do celebrate with some corn beef and cabbage, which is a great alternative. Nevertheless, for each meal we offer, we also decorate the break room specifically to the holiday that inspired it. You can also introduce holiday inspired games curated to get people interacting with one another and have some fun.

These monthly meals don't cost more than $200 per month if done right. It's a minimal investment of $2400 a year. But the return on investment is invaluable, based on the camaraderie it creates. These meals provide positive interaction, build productive relationships, and boost contributions and impact well beyond the initial investment. As mentioned at the start of this section, you need to be providing the basic time, tools, and training to your team first and foremost before this is truly going to have a positive impact, otherwise a pizza party can feel more like a slap in the face. I once saw a meme that drove this point home perfectly. It was a picture of the flex seal guy slapping his product on a sinking ship, and the flex seal represented a pizza party masking the problem with an ingenuine gesture. So don't go fail as a leader and then feel good about yourself because you were nice and bought pizza. Do your part, and then reward and unify through a communal meal monthly and the results will be well worth the investment made.

Kindness Wall

Have you ever heard the quote, "Throw Kindness Around Like Confetti." Well, inspired by this quote is something I have created in the past that is another great way to encourage positive change in the way people think and act. It's called the Kindness Wall. You may remember me saying earlier that quotes are only words unless we live by them, so with some chalkboard paint and a few chalk markers, I write the quote on a wall and inspire action.

The purpose of this wall is to encourage PDA. No, not public displays of affection, but rather public displays of appreciation!

How does it function, and what are its benefits? Don't worry, I will break it down for you. You start with some chalkboard paint and the quote on the wall in some cool cursive. Then comes the main artistic ingredient. I draw a whole bunch of confetti around the quote because, duh! Then you attach a post-it and pen holder to the wall. I usually use a plastic brochure holder. That way you can supply plenty of colorful post-its and sharpies to write with. On either side of the kindness quote you will want to write, "Write One" on the left side and "Take One" on the right side. That way, people engaging with the wall know what to do. The idea is that this wall is to inspire you to have an attitude of gratitude and spread kindness through encouraging words on post-its to your fellow employees. Whether it's a note from a manager to his team member, or a message from peer to peer, the positive effect from these genuine gestures is positively contagious.

The Kindness wall is a living wall. Meaning it's encouraged to take a post-it written for you, and write one in exchange. Then you put it in your desk, your locker, or your wallet to remind you that people care about you and that the work you're doing matters.

Now you might be thinking, "I remember having something similar to this back in the day at school." You're probably right. That's why you continue to hear me say that being inspired by the structure from your early years is a secret to cultural success. While there is a difference in the articulation and specifics of our encouragement now as an adult vs as a kid, the motivating and encouraging impact is the same if not more now.

I'm sure you have heard the phrase, "to praise in public and criticize in private." Well, here is a great opportunity for every employee on payroll to publicly praise one another; Encouraging not only an attitude of gratitude, but also encouraging others to continue the behaviors we want to see more of. That's why it's important to get out of the mindset that you are too old for juvenile initiatives like the kindness wall, as they truly benefit your business. It will make a lasting impact on your employees as people, well beyond their employment, and that's something we should all be striving for. The kindness wall creates familiarity, engagement, encouragement, support, care, and kindness. All things that this world and your people need more of in their life.

Thank you Cards

Similar to the Kindness Wall which is more public, I recommend introducing thank you cards for employees to share peer-to-peer, that provides a private avenue to show gratitude. I recommend you keep these cards located wherever paychecks are given out. Where the kindness wall creates a public display of appreciation, a thank you card is more personal and private.

The reason I provide this as an additional outlet of peer-to-peer communication and recognition is because sometimes what you want to thank someone for is not something you want to share with the world. Whether someone is going through challenges personally, at work, or at home, I want to encourage people to support and celebrate one another. There's just so many great things being done around the organization that go unnoticed unless written in a review or an email, that it's important to create multiple outlets for peer-to-peer recognition.

For example, if I was a houseman carrying a ton of chairs

down multiple flights of stairs because the elevator happened to break down that day, and you see me sweating and struggling and decide to stop what you are doing to help me, not only will I express my appreciation in the moment, but now I have an outlet to recognize your support and extra effort in a personalized handwritten note. That will have a greater and more rewarding impact on the person who decided to help than you may realize. Helping people feels good, but being recognized feels better. By having something like this encouraged in your culture, you not only increase acts of kindness, but you also increase recognition not just by the higher ups but by everyone.

Once the note is written it gets dropped in a box which gets later sorted and attached on the recipients paycheck as a nice surprise on Friday. That moment when they show up to pick up their paycheck and see a note they didn't know they were getting will put a huge smile on their face and put gratefulness in their heart. What this does is strengthens relationships, spreads appreciation and positivity, as well as continuing acts of kindness and the recognition of them.

It becomes a pay it forward kind of initiative. So if you receive a note from a fellow team member for jumping in and supporting someone, you then are expected to keep your eye out for others doing good deeds around the building and recognizing them for it. If everyone in your organization is walking around searching for the good instead of the bad, and doing more random acts of kindness for one another, then your culture will shift in a positive and profound way. It will become contagious, and that positive energy will spread from your people into the customer experience.

Annual Employee Party

My final recommended employee appreciation initiative is hosting an Annual Employee Party. This event does not need to break the bank but it does need to be well thought out and well executed. It also needs to happen every year regardless of your financial outcome. Because this event is about celebrating the journey and the people who joined you on it, not about profitability, although that can be celebrated, too, if it's achieved. Be sure to design it's theme and structure around your specific business and the interests of your employees.

The purpose of this annual event is to show genuine appreciation to your employees for the contributions and hard work that went into that year, celebrating not just the good days, but the bad days too because you were able to tackle them together. It creates a tradition that everyone in your organization looks forward to year after year, and is another positive interaction and memory built around fun family bonding. It's also an opportunity to create an experience that amplifies your company culture, and gets talked about around the building for months to come. While it's normal to think to keep employees uninvolved in planning such an event, it's important you provide an opportunity for people to get involved. Offer it out to any volunteers that have interest and want to showcase their skills.

This means if someone is skilled in event planning and coordinating, get them involved. If they are skilled in decorating, or are musically inclined get them involved. If they have connections to get door prizes get them involved. If they have relationships with vendors for donations get them involved. It may be for employees to enjoy but it's also important to remember to recognize people's interests and talents by providing them an outlet to showcase them through involvement in the event.

In order to engage your team members, your party planning needs to involve more than hiring a DJ and a caterer. Otherwise, the event won't last longer than dinner because they will scarf down some food and disappear. Your appreciation in this event needs to be shown and felt through well thought out and orchestrated activities, entertainment, food & beverage options, and awards and prizes. That way the night is full of fun and not limited in people's involvement.

From my experience, the event should kick-off with some low-key conversation starters that get people walking around the room and connecting with one another. A way to do this is by incorporating some trivia questions or who's who photo guessing games in the decor of your table settings. Providing a prize to whoever gets the most correct.

From a room design side of things, I recommend providing open soft seating where people can eat, drink, mingle and rest when needed. Make sure you incorporate these seating options throughout the action areas of the room to ensure the room flows and keeps engagement up as it fills up in that first hour.

A great way to continue the conversation beyond the event

and amplifying your company culture is by having a photo
booth. This doesn't have to be an expensive vendor booth,
it can be an inexpensive backdrop from Amazon and an
iPad. No one is going to remember the photobooth guy
anyway, so don't waste your money. The part that matters
most is that you are creating a space for all employees to
engage with one another regardless of what department
they work in to have a little fun, creating memories and
mementos to be reminisced about later that night and for
days and weeks to come.

Something to keep in mind when planning this event is
that not everyone attending is nominated for an award.
Since a large chunk of the event is giving out awards, you
may see a strong lack of interest by those uninvolved if
you're not careful. The idea is to keep those not watching
or winning excited and still engaged. A great way to do this
is by creating a game of chance that everyone participates
in throughout the night, which provides an opportunity to
win some prizes along the way. Whether it's a treasure
chest that everyone gets a key to, or a locker that everyone
gets a combo to try out, the idea is to provide everyone an
opportunity to get involved and potentially win a prize.
Prizes can range from gift cards, to headphones, to 50inch
TVs. Just make sure you showcase all the available prizes
to win on a table near the game ensuring visibility and
peaked interest. Oh, and make sure to remind people
about this game of chance throughout the night, otherwise
they may get distracted and miss their chance to win it all.
You will realize that many people in your organization
have never won anything in their entire life, so this game
of chance can create some super special moments. So be
on the lookout.

Speaking of winning stuff, everyone will be anticipating who the Employee of the Year and Manager of the Year winners are. I will discuss how you choose a winner in greater detail in a later chapter. But, I recommend not limiting your awards to just 2. That's why I typically throw in some superlative awards as well. Similar to the ones we all had in our school yearbook. Superlative awards can range from Best Dressed, to Caffeine Addict, to Most likely to be Famous. Whatever you choose, make sure it still represents your company and culture. These should be voted on prior to the event by their peers and given out prior to the big awards. This will keep people engaged, smiling, and laughing along the way.

Once all the awards have been presented its time to dance! As mentioned, getting a dj and caterer isn't the only thing you should do, but you also shouldn't skimp out on a DJ either. Finding a trusted DJ is important because just like at a wedding, if the music doesn't get people out of their seats and on the dance floor it's a mood killer and people will clear out. So invest in a good one and play the music your team wants to hear. Then let the magic happen and join the fun. I also recommend, as corny as they are, making sure your DJ puts some of those line dancing songs like the *cupid shuffle*, and *cha cha slide* in his mix. These songs get people to come together in unison and there is great subtle value to that. Any opportunity to unify your team even if it's over a funny dance is worth capitalizing on.

One last thing I recommend is throwing some money at a photographer. Like I said before, skip out on the photobooth guy, but hiring a photographer on the other hand allows you to capture those candid moments of laughter and fun as people dance the night away. Events like this come once a year but photos from them last forever. And photos can be a tool to continue to tell a story of genuine appreciation that builds your culture and team from the inside out.

In Conclusion

In writing this chapter, it was my goal to provide you with genuine and sustainable employee appreciation initiatives that ensure your people feel valued and appreciated. I also wanted to make sure you understood the value behind them, and not just do as I say but feel inspired to create your own version. Through consistent recognition and reward, your employees will undoubtedly do more to improve your business. Taking action to add initiatives such as these will continue to strengthen your internal relationships, ensuring your people feel loved, served, and cared for unlike any place they've worked or called home before.

4 ONGOING COMMUNICATION

Communication is a key to every business's success, yet we all struggle to find ways to improve it. Unfortunately, without taking time to research best practices and attempting to improve through trial and error we won't find much progress. Not to mention, the process of learning through failure takes time and who has extra of that lying around. Lucky for you, I've done my fair share of learning through failure when it comes to communication, so I'm going to help you skip a couple steps and avoid the fall. That process of falling down and getting back up taught me that communication comes in many forms. In order to ensure your communication is received and understood by everyone in your organization you must deliver it in all four phases. Otherwise, the inconsistencies in one area of communication will contaminate the view of the whole, forcing it to be viewed as a failed system.

The four phases of communication that need to be

incorporated in your daily operation include verbal, non-verbal, written, and visual. In order to stress the importance of consistency and the strength of all four phases when done together, I want you to picture each of those phases written on the legs of a chair. Each leg represents a phase that together is the foundation of your organizational success. All four phases are needed to ensure support and balance in the daily operation. In this example, if you were to sit down on that chair and represent the productivity and efficiency of your hotel, what do you think would happen if I came over and kicked a leg out from under you? The outcome would be pretty obvious, right. The organization (you) that was once well balanced and supported would quickly and abruptly come crashing down to the ground. Dramatic or not, the point I'm trying to make is that you need to make a conscious effort to provide all 4 phases in your operation in order to have long term success. It's not good enough to just check all the boxes. So allow me to provide you my best practices to ensure strength in all 4 phases.

Verbal

Verbal communication is when we engage in speaking with others. If you notice I used the word engaging. That is the most important element to verbal communication other than consistency. If you have ever heard Ben Stein speak, you know he is probably one of the least engaging speakers you will ever hear. You may remember him as the Clear Eyes guy, or from Ferris Bueller's Day Off as the monotone teacher who says, "Bueller", over and over. Needless to say, when you speak you don't want to sound like that guy. As a leader, it is your responsibility to articulate purpose, values, and strategies that enable the financial responsibility and accountability of your leaders. If you are not engaging when speaking, by drawing attention and interest to what you speak on, it will not be retained or acted on.

The way to do that is to have passion, belief, and understanding about what you are trying to convey. That way your team will hear what you said and go do something about it. Now being engaging and speaking with passion and belief takes practice. There's no quick fix. You're just gonna have to work on it. But if every decision you make is what's best for your employees, then articulating purpose, and impact will be easy to do. Doing what's best for your people is something we can all believe in. And if you truly believe in the power of that, your people will feel it too.

Verbal communication should be done every single day. There is no communication phase more powerful than verbal. The purpose of this is to speak things into existence and speak people into action. Through engaging with others one-on-one, at huddle, in monthly department meetings, or in a quarterly town hall, you can inspire and motivate people to not only be better themselves, but come together and be better together. That's an exciting opportunity we all share, so don't you dare take it for granted.

I always find it interesting how we have these opportunities throughout the day to speak and inspire others, yet we rarely use them to make a greater impact. But I'm telling you right now it is your responsibility to intentionally think through and deliver motivation and expectations daily. Through repetition you will ensure your team members not only understand but also begin to create the habits necessary to improve and build upon what you are communicating. Whether one-on-one or with a group, begin to take these opportunities more seriously and use repetition to be more verbally intentional today.

Non-Verbal

I have a quote tattooed on my arm that explains non-verbal communication better than I can, so I figured I would start by sharing it.

"The first thing you say, is rarely ever spoken."

What this quote means to me personally is that we only get one first impression and we are typically judged by how we look and act prior to ever speaking a word. How this applies to you is this. What we do while we speak, often says more than the actual words themselves. Non-verbal communication includes facial expressions, body movement, posture, eye contact, and engagement. There's that word again. Let me show you what I mean. Let's say you are reviewing new leadership expectations at your monthly meeting and you are sitting, not standing, head in hand, reading off a paper, speaking in a monotone. Do you think these non-verbal cues are exciting and engaging to the group? I don't think so. I know if I was in attendance I would quickly become uninterested and disengaged. This is why it's important for you to be more conscious of your non-verbal communication.

It's also absolutely crucial you lead by example. Actions

speak louder than words. As an example, let's say in a meeting you led a few days back, you set clear expectations to your team that as you start the final month of the year, everyone across all departments needs to be disciplined in following the budget, cutting costs and limiting any unnecessary expenditures. Yet not even a week later, the employee entryway is lined with boxes from Amazon with your name on it with your new office furniture. Don't you think that sends a very contradictory non-verbal message? It tells your team to do as I say not as I do, which as I've explained, removes any motivation to follow through on what is asked of them. Even if the purchase was approved or came off a budgeted line, it still sends the wrong message. This then creates a culture of anything goes. If you're not willing to do what you're asking, why would your team? Hold yourself and your team accountable to leading by example and following through on what is verbally communicated. Otherwise, morale and motivation will be down for the count, and there will be no one to blame but yourself.

The other side to non-verbal communication is picking up on non-verbal cues. Pay attention to the non-verbal communication going on around you. If you are in a meeting and you feel like you're energized and engaging, delivering your version of the Gettysburg Address, but your team is avoiding eye contact, sighing, or yawning then you're not connecting with your audience. At which point, you should be prepared to pivot and adjust your approach to better grab their attention. Don't worry, I will be reviewing ways to do so in the chapters up ahead. But for now, let's move on to written communication.

Written

Whether it's an email, a text, or a memo all forms of written communication have the same purpose and that is to distribute information in a clear and concise manner. As simple as that sounds, its often not achieved. Employees need to know what to expect day to day, week to week, and month to month. So, if you do not currently have a system in place to plan that far ahead or communicate those expectations, look no further I got your back.

Let's start with daily written communication. In my experience in hotels, there can be a lot happening in one day. From guests arriving and departing, to VIPs, to events and their location, the long list can be daunting at times. In order to keep your team up to date on today's current events, I recommend implementing something called Daily Deets. This two-sided flash card size sheet that fits in the palm of your hand is created by the overnight team and put by the time clock for employees to take and be aware of what to expect on each given day. This is an important tool as it also allows your team to be well informed and helps them look knowledgeable and prepared when communicating to guests. This is another example of how putting your employees' needs first (being informed) helps directly impact your guests in a positive way.

Another great way to distribute information to your employees and guests alike is via text. Nowadays everyone has a smartphone. So if there is something everyone should know, the quickest form of communication is through text messaging. There is a great business texting software I highly recommend called Zingle that provides you the ability to send real-time personalized SMS engagement. Whether you want to message a guest to tell them their room is ready, or send out an all-employee message informing them the pool is closing due to inclimate weather, you have the flexibility to do so. This tool has been invaluable to me and all businesses who choose to use it through my recommendation. Not only does it bridge the gap and improve operations, but it also provides a great opportunity to communicate one-on-one from GM to employee on any given day. It's a leader's job to develop those relationships and a strategy to stay connected and this software is a relatable way to do so. Whether it's a birthday or anniversary text, a feel better text, or a text sending your condolences, this is a tool that can be utilized to show care and support to your people wherever they are. It provides you with the best opportunity to engage, and start a dialogue when they may need it most.

The next form of written or really typed communication I want to touch on is via email. Emails have great value when they come from the top. They also can save a lot of time. If you are a GM, send more personal emails out. Your people want to hear from you. I do this in the same capacity as I do text, just not as often. It's not about overkill, it's about an intentional effort to connect directly with your people showing them you are available and care. Additionally, It's important to know as a leader that you shouldn't wait until a meeting to communicate stuff, and you shouldn't always create a meeting to do so either. I'm sure you've all heard people say, "That meeting could have been an email." If it's being said, they are usually right. Communication is needed all day everyday. So finding creative and engaging ways to do so is key.

If you wait for a meeting to discuss issues, it may either be irrelevant by the time you get around to it or forgotten because it wasn't written down and you got too busy to remember. A great way to solve this is a quick email. For example, if you are in a high-level meeting and you are discussing events or operational changes that immediately affect your team members, I highly recommend each member of the meeting taking notes and sending a recap of what applies to their teams via email. In the email, you'll explain what to expect as well as inform them that you will be following up later that day to discuss and answer any questions. By doing this, you create accountability; not just for yourself to circle back and check in, but also for your leaders to ensure understanding and seamless implementation. Waiting for a meeting or forgetting to communicate is no longer an excuse. Keep your people in the loop by simply sending an email and following up.

Lastly, in regards to written communication, I highly recommend introducing a monthly newsletter into the mix. By creating a strong line of communication among employees through a newsletter, you not only promote company updates, but also boost morale, and productivity. Your people want to hear from you and want to be in the know. Having a strong newsletter also keeps your employees connected to your mission which motivates and moves you forward in a positive way.

There are 5 major reasons I encourage you to start a newsletter in your organization. The first being that it provides a platform to share important company information whether its procedural, an upcoming event, or exciting company growth. Second, it allows you an opportunity to recognize and share birthdays, anniversaries, new hires, and employee of the month. Third, it can give your employees a chance to contribute their voice and perspective by creating a small column specifically for employees to submit their own ideas. Fourth, it can be used as an internal marketing tool to expand mission and brand awareness. Lastly, it can keep your team updated on your financial status and how their contributions impact achieving your goals. These 5 reasons individually are important, but collectively in one source of communication are unstoppable. The newsletter helps close the gap and once designed, is easy to maintain month after month.

Visual

Being a visual learner myself, I understand and appreciate this form of communication the most. We have become a very visually driven society, and so it's important we use this in a positive and productive way. Television, social media, and all these other platforms each use imagery to sell products and services. And while at first thought you aren't looking to sell anything to your employees, it's important you shift your thinking and use these visual communication opportunities as internal marketing for your organization. Specifically, use visual platforms as a way to promote your company mission, objectives, and goals in an engaging way, ultimately creating familiarity, loyalty, and brand advocacy from the inside out. The idea is to be intentional in the things you promote and broadcast internally. So I'm going to provide you with some proven ways to improve visual communication and increase engagement and involvement.

Introducing a photo slideshow in your back of house areas has been one of the most visually engaging and rather mesmerizing things to watch progress through my experience in building company culture. Unfortunately, more often than not when mentioning this idea to hotels, they rarely realize the value of photo taking and tend to have a very limited supply. So if this is you, be better prepared by keeping your phone handy at all employee functions. The idea is to then use those photos taken over time to create a powerpoint slide show that you broadcast on all back of house TVs. The purpose is to show and remind your employees of all the fun and good they accomplish together. Whether it's photos of all hands-on deck moments, special occasions, offsite events, they all have significant value.

The reason you cover the walls of your house with family photos, is the same reason you need to do so at work. It promotes a feeling of love, value, and belonging. It creates togetherness. When I first implemented this at a hotel, it was in an area where we hosted our daily huddle. So I would sit and watch at the start and end of huddle as everyone's energy and engagement would go up as they watched the slideshow, smiling and talking about the memories as they went by. Many times we would all just sit and watch the slideshow through to the end which was hundreds and hundreds of photos. Needless to say, the positive impact of this visual form of communication was instant and really made a difference. It communicated to all who watched it that they are loved, valued, and belong.

Another element of visual communication can be done through posters. Posters can communicate upcoming events, training, and celebrations. No I'm not talking about posters like you had on your walls in middle school taped up and tacky. I'm talking about well designed and thought out marketing tools to engage your employees, which should be strategically placed in sleek snap frames across all back of house areas. An amazing tool I call my secret weapon, that makes internal marketing design easy, is an app called Canva. Canva is a graphic design platform that has become my go to for all internal marketing needs. Canva keeps it simple with their easy drag and drop design features, custom templates, and stock content. It allows you, an inexperienced graphic designer, to create amazing internal marketing designs like a pro. Posters like these have become a staple in improving communication in every culture I've been a part of. They allow you to promote upcoming events like Coffee & Questions (which I will review later), Monthly Meal gatherings in the breakroom, and even the Annual Employee Party. They also allow you to recognize Employee of the Month nominations and the winners. They can even be designed as sign-up sheets for one-on-ones with the GM. Posters are a constant visual reminder to employees, keeping them knowledgeable, engaged, and involved. So download Canva and start creating your visual communications today.

In Conclusion

We communicate continually throughout each and every day. We do it in multiple ways, and many times without even thinking. However, I encourage you to think about how you are communicating by being more intentional about it. Remember, there are four pillars of communication and if one is removed the house comes crashing down. The biggest issue with communication is the illusion that it has happened. Remove the illusion through intention by creating strong verbal, non-verbal, written, and visual communication daily.

5 MEETINGS MATTER

Meetings truly make or break a team and the outcome determines a team's long term success or failure, yet no one ever teaches us how to properly and effectively run one. That's why in this chapter I will provide you with all the training you need to successfully run a meeting that not only improves collaboration and productivity, but also leaves people feeling energized and involved. Before we get into the steps for sustainable success, let's first start with what not to do.

Have you ever been in a meeting where you are talked at for an hour? Worse yet, have you ever been in a meeting where everyone is at each other's necks and the tension can be cut with a knife before it even starts? How about those meetings about meetings, or you know, those meetings that could have just been an email. Having a manager host a meeting just to have one doesn't help anyone either.

The funny thing about all these examples is that we've all

been a part of them, hated the experience, and yet follow the same framework as we grow and become responsible for conducting meetings ourselves. That's because they are our point of reference. Observation was the only training we got on how to conduct a meeting. So the vicious cycle continues, because no one takes the time to research, learn, and adjust. They just go with what they know. Maybe it's because we don't have the time to, or maybe it's because we don't *make* the time to. Either way it's time to change the cycle.

Companies don't see the value in training their leaders, especially on something as simple as how to conduct a meeting. They just expect you to know. They pay you enough don't they? This thinking has a negative impact on your operation. It's the blind leading the blind as they say.

Too many times in organizations needing my help, I find meetings to be a panel to cast blame and identify problems. We need to be problem solvers, not problem identifiers. Problems will always remain problems if everyone just goes around pointing them out. If this behavior is part of your current culture and meeting agenda you must address it and change it immediately, because that is a surefire way to kill a culture. Take it from a guy who has seen it first hand and had to fix it. That is not the way to run a meeting or a business. You must be better, and I'm here to help. So now that you understand the problem let's get into how to fix it.

Consistency

Let's start with the most important word in building anything that matters, consistency. You must be consistent in how and when you deliver a meeting in order to see positive results. Consistency builds strength over time through muscle memory, just like with physical exercise. So the best place to start when looking to improve consistency with meetings is your calendar. Often your operation can pull you in 7 directions at a time which can lead to rescheduled or inconsistently scheduled meetings. This kills your momentum and progress. To avoid this, simply schedule your monthly meetings the same time every single month. That way there's no question when to show up. I recommend the second Tuesday or Wednesday of each month, but that's just me. The next thing that needs to be consistent is the structure of the meeting. That way, not only does everyone know when to show up, but they also know what to expect and how to be prepared when they do. So the remainder of this chapter will describe the general agenda that brought me success when conducting a productive meeting.

Start with stories

I mentioned stories before when I introduced you to daily huddle. Storytelling is a powerful and relatable tool to bring people together. That's why you should kick off every meeting with a sharing session because sharing is caring. Going around the room allows each person to share personal or team wins, or better yet, recognize someone else's extra effort over the last 30 days. What this does is kick off the meeting with positive vibes and allows people to connect through being open with one another. It also starts the meeting with everyone engaging and not being talked at. In the hotel industry specifically, many team members rarely cross paths more than a few times a month, so swapping stories at the start of each monthly meeting helps unify them.

Once the group has shared their, stories, it's time you share yours. Then segue into the teams collective successes since you last were together. Whether it's the departments raving reviews, saving 20% on expenses, or exceeding budgeted revenues, it's important to recognize the group for their collective effort while also helping them understand that what they do daily, impacts these things more than they realize. Then recognize individual successes. Whether it's celebrating attendance, involvement in the community, or employee of the month nomination or win, recognizing people in a public setting like this articulates purpose and helps the team celebrate victories and understand what you and the company values. It's an opportunity to show the best in them and inspire others to be better themselves.

Listen to them

In order to keep the theme of not talking *at* your team, next I move on to discussing challenges and allowing the team an open forum to discuss things that are holding them back from greatness. It's a time where I simply listen to them. Because there's no better person to tell me what's not working then the people in the trenches on a daily basis. At the end of the day, every person on this planet wants to be heard, so this time, during the meeting, is vital to your success as a manager and as a team. When listening, do not listen with the intent to speak. Otherwise you won't truly be engaged in listening or caring what others have to say. I know this well because it is an area of opportunity for me. I don't always allow people to finish when speaking because I tend to feel an urgency to say what's on the tip of my tongue, but this behavior is detrimental to your leadership and team success. So take notes from someone who is working on it themselves and has seen the negative effects it has. When you listen, listen with your heart and care what each person has brought to your attention.

When we start this part of the meeting, I ask that if you have a problem you want to discuss, you must also come prepared with a solution. It may not be the solution we decide on in the end, but having these tough conversations will inspire new ideas on how to work smarter, simpler, and safer. It's important that people begin to see obstacles as opportunities and become problem solvers not just identifiers. Anyone can bring an issue to light but it can be harmful, whether intentional or not. It's much more fulfilling and impactful to transform your thinking into finding solutions. Allow these tough conversations to inspire bigger and better ideas through collaboration.

Once you have *heard* the challenges and discussed as a group the solutions you are all willing to commit to, then you can bring up anything of urgent concern that you may have observed since last together. Provide your own suggested solutions, and create collective responsibility. In these sessions as tough conversations come up, it's key to steer the conversation in a way that is productive and holds everyone accountable. Over time, this will increase involvement in the discussion and rid out things that have held your team back from greatness.

At the end of this segment of the agenda, I review

anything discussed last time on our to-do-list for improvement and encourage consistency while celebrating any accomplishments. We then add any new items discussed to the list, and put completion dates to ensure we deliver on our promise to one another. If it's something that can be owned by someone individually I will offer it up, otherwise I get a group commitment and we move on.

Team Building

I am a big proponent of team building activities. Similar to the ice breakers we all did back in school, these quick and efficient exercises provide a positive perspective by teaching your team through active and immersive trial and error. It creates that aha moment that teaches without you having to say a word. Team building doesn't always have to be a game though. It can be providing a scenario and having groups come to a solution together. There are many approaches you can take, but whatever you decide to do it must be done together. The best way to learn and grow is to be uncomfortable. This is why many people do not reach their potential, chase after their dreams, or enjoy team building. It's time to get your people out of their comfort zone and grow better together. Allow me to provide you an example exercise that I have used in the past for communication and collaboration that may inspire ideas of your own. I've found great success with this and it involves only a roll of duct tape, a chair, and some finger support.

The most recent occasion I used this activity was with a group that was super dysfunctional. Their manager had recently been fired and in his absence, they all individually decided they should be in charge and tell people what to do. No one person had stepped up to lead. Everyone just demanded to be heard and assumed the power of authority. This created a hostile work environment and made it so that everyone was at their wits end with one another. In the day to day operations when challenges would arise, instead of coming together they fell apart. That's where I came in. It was time to teach them that they needed each other and that the way they communicated needed to change, but because telling people what to do was the issue at hand I knew I couldn't just tell them to shape up or ship out. They were so against hearing criticism from one another they would never listen to it from me. At least not yet. They needed to figure it out themselves. That's why I turned to team building to do the teaching for me. This would guide them to understanding they can and need to be better together.

The way the exercise is executed is that all 5 people involved need to stand up and form a circle, each person puts one index finger in towards one another forming what looks like a sun. You then place a chair outside the group circle, and a roll of duct tape on top of their fingers. Their fingers act as a support system and a way of transportation for the roll of tape. You then let the team know their objective is to get that tape from where they stand, down and over safely to the chair below. What happens next gives everyone a good laugh. When you give the team the go ahead to get started, everyone just starts moving in different directions, but they quickly learn the importance of teamwork and communication. Their lack of it, has everyone giggling in fear of dropping the tape only 2 seconds in.

These laughs were important in my case because tension was high between the group to start. With the challenges presented in the game as is, I wanted to raise the stakes and see how they would perform under more pressure. Under pressure, this group typically fell apart. The variable was this; I would occasionally simulate a scenario where someone in the group would need to remove themselves for a short period of time, 6 seconds at most, as if they were being pulled, as managers do, to help elsewhere. For example, I told the F&B supervisor the diner is getting slammed and someone called out, please remove your finger in an attempt to assist. Mind you, the team needed to quickly adjust in her absence and still pursue their goal of lowering the tape down to the chair. But her absence changed the balance of things which created difficulty. Then I selected the Security Supervisor to remove his finger saying there's been a call out and you need to work the door. This left 3 people out of 5 to support the tape due to callouts. These people who removed their fingers would stay removed until "coverage came in" to relieve them. This may only last a few seconds in the game but the impact shakes up the balance of the team.

Through this process you may lose your lead communicator of the group to a scenario, and so the others need to step up and adjust accordingly. Through this process you may lose someone who is quieter but has helped balance and steer the group more than you realize. So as the scenarios continued to shake things up, it was interesting to see how everyone adjusted along the way. Ultimately, this exercise takes the team a few tries based on the difficulty of the balancing act and unexpected variables. But the difficulty is what teaches the team through trial and error the importance of togetherness and communication. After they accomplish the goal you celebrate and sit down to discuss what they personally learned through the experience.

In this specific case for me, the team realized that the duct tape represented the operation as a whole. That in order to be successful, they all needed to do their parts while also having collective responsibility. They realized that any one individual is important, but collectively they are unstoppable. We discussed the importance of communication and having one voice. When variables happen, this team can get through it if they work together as one. This exercise did not solve all their problems and it didn't change things overnight, but it was the introduction to recognizing and resolving their problem. It helped them understand how each of them was part of the problem, and could commit to be part of the solution. Over time it changed for the better and that's the power of team building.

This is why I highly recommend you introduce similar exercises into your monthly meeting itinerary, because they create friendly competition and break up the monotony of, a meeting. Research some ideas based on your team's current needs, and try one out in your next meeting. They will unify your team regardless of the outcome.

Remind & Rate

As your meeting comes to an end, similar to how a coach gives a speech after a team practice, you need to bring it all together by motivating your team to continue on this productive path together. In your close out conversation, you need to summarize and remind everyone what was discussed and accomplished and what your group goals are after you all leave the room. You must understand how you make them feel throughout the meeting, but especially at the end, dictates their energy and effort as they exit. So take this time to remind them of their purpose and contributions. Be constructive yet motivating promoting the behaviors you want to see more of and give them reason to do so. And as you finish your spiel and the meeting comes to a close, ask your people for honest feedback. Rating the meeting from 1-10 and allowing them to provide suggestions on how it can continue to get better. By doing this, you build a foundation of accountability and betterment which will progress your team's contribution and impact.

In Conclusion

Meetings have a major impact on the short and long term success of a team. Leaving every meeting with solutions to take action on is a key to their success. There were a lot of other important takeaways sprinkled throughout this chapter that I want to make sure are clearly spelled out for you to take note of for implementation. So again, in order to run a successful meeting you will need to ensure the following items are included:

- Share stories
- Celebrate Successes
- Set Goals and Update them on Status
- Discuss Challenges and ask them for Feedback/Solutions
- Keep it Constructive and Productive

- Do something active/immersive (Team Building and/or Training)
- Remind them of their contribution
- Recognize & Reward
- Articulate purpose and encourage them as they exit

Whether these items are in this order or exactly as I expressed them in this chapter really doesn't matter. The only thing that truly matters is that you take the list above and construct your team's needed version of it. If you do that, your team will notice your effort and adjustment and will become more engaged and interested in participating as you move forward.

6 CONSIDER & ACT ON SUGGESTIONS

Have you ever approached your manager with an idea, to either have them dismiss it or later find it in the trash? I have. Unfortunately, in this story I wasn't the one with the idea, I was the manager. I had a passionate employee come to me once with an idea she had worked hard on about becoming more eco-friendly around the hotel. And while it was a great idea, and applicable to our operation, it was delivered to me at a time when I was overwhelmed, and I just didn't have the mental capacity to appreciate it. The timing of her delivery had me listening with the intent to respond rather than understand, which later led to me tossing the paperwork about it in the trash on my way out the door that day. As a young leader I was naive, and had no idea the negative impact or implications of my actions. I told her I'd consider it at the moment, but my lack of attentiveness created a lack of interest which then led to the careless tossing of it in a trash can, where she would later find it. Talk about a punch to the gut from your manager. My actions not only diminished her morale and motivation, but greatly affected her feelings about me and the organization. Her negative experience was then communicated throughout the team and it spread like wildfire. I messed up and owned it, but the damage was done.

I share this story with you for two reasons. The first reason is because I want you to understand the impact of your decisions as a leader holds great weight, and that they can dramatically impact your team in both positive and negative ways. You need to keep perspective and appreciate the moment. The second reason is that I want you to know I've made many mistakes throughout my journey just as you will, but the key is to not repeat those mistakes by learning from them and using them to improve.

This situation helped groom me as a manager and leader. By learning through failure, I decided to not allow this to happen again. Therefore, implemented ways to ensure suggestions were not only encouraged, but also considered and acted on.

When it comes to suggestions, it's important to start by setting expectations with your team. Letting them know that while you can't always act on everything they suggest, you will always consider it. If you currently have no system in place to ensure your people's suggestions are made, it's time you start. In this chapter, I will review 4 different ways to ensure your employees' voices get heard and considered on an ongoing basis, as well as the best way to communicate from the top down that suggestions were heard, considered, and whether they were or were not acted on. Just taking a suggestion isn't good enough. You need to do something with it and make sure it's communicated, otherwise assumptions will be made and trust will break down.

Suggestion Box

Let's start with the simplest way to encourage suggestions: a suggestion box! You can usually find one on amazon for as little as $20 and even though it's a small investment, it yields great returns. I typically put the suggestion box by the time clock as it's a place guaranteed to be seen by every hourly employee at minimum twice a day. The box is self-explanatory, but I still recommend writing an encouraging note on the box to motivate your employees to engage. The most important element to this concept is not the box itself but rather the data collected and the results. That's why I recommend putting a bulletin board in your break room with a section for suggestions, broken out in two parts for all to see. One should be the suggestions made, and the other should be actions taken.

The suggestion box should be checked weekly and reviewed with your executive team to be updated monthly. This will keep your leadership team in the loop of what ideas, concerns, and solutions were made, to then be discussed collectively. If for any reason a suggestion is not able to be acted on, it's important to still put it in the Action Taken section of the bulletin board to explain why you won't be moving forward. Otherwise, the person who wrote it will feel dismissed and lose faith in the system. This will then become negatively contagious across the entire team, similar to the story I shared.

It's also important to have an open mind when reading these suggestions. Line level employees are the ones in the trenches, and have first hand experience in the day to day operation. If they are taking the time to suggest improvements, it means they really care and you shouldn't take their willingness to share for granted. Therefore it is imperative you have an open mind to allow yourself the opportunity to learn from those around you, especially the ones seeing operational deficiency first hand.

From a comfortability standpoint, one of the nice things about a suggestion box is it provides a confidential, non-confrontational way to express one's ideas. Not to say a conversation about improving should ever get confrontational, but it eases the mind of those providing the suggestion and removes unnecessary interaction. It keeps things simple and avoids anyone taking offense, and rather focuses on getting advice. Some may want to talk directly to the source, so it's pivotal you provide additional suggestion options to ensure the way your people feel comfortable communicating is available to them.

Coffee & Questions

Have you ever held back saying something to your brother or sister in fear of the consequences, but when you're in the family room with your parents present, you muster up the guts to say it? The reason you do that is because you know your parents will support you, which removes the fear holding you back from saying it. The most common reasons people don't speak up is they either fear rejection, fear the truth, or believe nothing will change. When surrounded by like minded and trusted people, it creates a comfortability and a confidence in them to speak up because they are supported, just like being in the room with your parents. That is how Coffee & Questions came about.

Coffee & Questions provides a scheduled one hour slot each month for employees to voluntarily join me and members of my executive team for coffee to ask any questions or provide any suggestions they may have. This is a super relaxed gathering, but provides an opportunity to gain trust, remove barriers, and build relationships to better your business.

This initiative will take some time to gain attendance because out of those three major reasons people don't speak up, the most prominent is always belief nothing will change. So you will need to work hard to build trust with those few who do attend and follow through on what you say you will do. Then you must make an effort to spread the word and encourage others to do the same.

Each session gives your staff a chance to ask you and your team questions on the spot, that if answered well, will gain their confidence and trust in you. You should also come prepared to ask the attendees relevant questions of your own, in hopes to get answers to unresolved issues. It gives you a platform to get answers just as much as your people.

Like I mentioned in the last chapter, verbal communication is the most impactful of the 4 major types. It allows you to inspire action. If you are intentional with this one hour slot of time each month, it can make a major difference over time. It provides your employees a platform to voice their opinions and get things resolved. It also provides you a platform to continue to articulate purpose, values, and belief in what you do and why you do it. And if done well, those in attendance will be inspired to continue to come and communicate to others the value it brings.

One-on-Ones

While some people are comfortable speaking in a group setting with others there to support, many prefer to speak not only in private, but confidentially. That is why I recommend you also introduce your own version of one-on-ones as an additional way to ensure your employees voices are heard and considered.

While I make sure my employees know I am always available to them 7 days a week, I typically hash out time specifically for employees to schedule one-on-ones with me quarterly. By scheduling these in the middle of the quarter, it allows enough time between them to create needed conversation, while also allowing enough time to fix things before the quarter ends. They should also be conducted in a private place whether in your office or tucked away in the corner of your lobby somewhere.

One-on-ones in my experience should go the length of a week, providing sign-up slots for employees to choose from across 5 days. I also recommend being available for both day and night sessions. This creates an opportunity for all three shifts to get that personal time with you they may not normally get. By making yourself available to your people when it's convenient not for you, but for them, goes a long way in their eyes. For example, it's always going to be tough to connect with your overnight team unless you stay over at the hotel, so if you come in at 7am to meet them on the tail end of their shift to catch up, they will greatly appreciate your willingness to do so. On the other hand, if your typical schedule has you end at 6pm most days, then schedule yourself later in the day once or twice that week of one-on-ones to be available in the evening hours for those who work 3p-11p shifts. As a leader, we serve our employees, not the other way around, so by creating flexibility in your schedule to accommodate them your actions speak this truth.

One-on-ones can be in two forms, organic and formal. Which way you go depends on the circumstances. If you're new to a role, I recommend a more formal format. Come prepared to not only assess the current way of things, but more importantly to get to know them personally and take notes. See below for the questions I use to formally get to know the people and the business at the start of a new role.

Personal:

Tell me about yourself?

When is your birthday? Do you like cake? What kind?

Favorite Food?

Where are you from?

What's your favorite sports team, music, or movie?

What are your goals? Short term, long term?

What are your hobbies, what do you like to do outside

of work?

Business:

Tell me about your experiences working here? What matters to you?

Are there clear expectations for you and your role on the team?

Do you have the materials and tools needed to be successful?

Do you have an opportunity to do what you do best everyday?

In the last 7 days have you received recognition or praise for a job well done?

Does your supervisor care about you as a person?

Is there someone at work who encourages your development?

Tell me your hopes and dreams for your future here?

What do I need to do to help you be more effective?

These questions are then used to improve the operation and have documentation about who likes what. That way, come birthday time, you are ahead of the game, and are able to surprise them with a gift they had forgotten you spoke about. This shows you care about them as an individual and creates trust through your attention to detail.

On the other hand, if you are months or years into a role and decide to schedule one-on-ones, I suggest a more fluid approach to one-on-ones. This fluid approach allows the employee to dictate the direction and development of the conversation. Even though you're not writing down every answer like you did in the formal approach, still make sure you are always prepared with a notepad handy to jot things down and review later. Organic one-on-ones should be relaxed and casual. These conversations provide the best results because they put the employee at ease, improving willingness to speak freely and discuss what's really going on.

When you complete a one-on-one, it's important you thank them for their time and their honesty, not the other way around. Then discuss whether they prefer you keep it between the two of you, or use it to improve it and discuss it with others to make change as a team. Employee trust is vital, so make sure you follow through on that part.

You will also want to be careful that you don't become emotionally driven by what's discussed in one-on-ones. For example, if you just hosted a one-on-one where you were told by a supervisor that her manager treats her unfairly and that he isn't good with people management and then emotionally decided to confront him about it, you will undoubtedly create a hostile work environment. Not only does this create tension between that manager and the employee who said it, but it also breaks down the trust and support that manager has with you. My recommendation on how to avoid this is to take notes, collect all the information, and then make a decision on how to best move forward, as long as the employee doesn't want to keep it confidential. Otherwise, you will begin jumping to conclusions, and making rash decisions that begin breaking down bonds in your team instead of building them. The key is to be supportive, encouraging, and empathetic. This allows these one-on-ones to not start a revolution, but rather create resolution. If done well, and in the way explained, this form of suggestion and intimate communication can build stronger relationships through trust by listening and delivering on promises. Remember to value their time and their feedback as it is a gift, and should be treated as such.

Employee Survey

A fourth and final opportunity to promote employee feedback is through a strategic survey. Unlike the first three initiatives that were voluntary, an employee survey done bi-annually is mandatory, meaning every employee on payroll gets involved. An employee survey empowers your team to provide valued feedback. It ensures all voices are heard, and helps them have a positive impact in navigating your organization's improvement.

An employee survey should be very strategic in asking questions that provide insights into employee satisfaction. This helps you to learn about their perspective on their compensation, your policies, scheduling, etc, as well as better understanding whether the basic time, tools, and training is available and provided. Ultimately, this measures engagement, motivation, commitment and morale.

A survey helps you gauge an organization in the moment and over time. Ideally there should be questions that are asked consistently from survey to survey for comparison purposes. But questions can be added and removed as needed based on your team's needs at a given time.

Implementing a survey has a lot of upside, but if it's not done consistently or used to improve things, it will just become another way to break down trust in your team. Once the survey is completed, similar to all the other forms of suggestion mentioned, you must put your notes together and assess it question by question. Use each one to develop a plan of action that improves any and all areas of opportunity over time. Then create and share your roadmap with your people. Whether you choose to communicate your plan for action on your employee bulletin board, by the time clock, or via email, it must be done in a way that creates an exciting vision for a better tomorrow, expressing your gratitude for their involvement and for being part of something bigger.

In Conclusion

The greatest impact of suggestion is not just in providing a voice to your people, but rather from the actions taken because each voice was heard. Similar to my story in the beginning of this chapter, if you get feedback or suggestions from an employee and fail to use it, fail to follow up, or fail to communicate and show results, you will completely destroy morale and motivation in your organization. That is why it is vital to your leadership's survival to listen, learn, and *leadershift* in order to better your culture. By using the 4 suggestion tools discussed in this chapter, you not only provide a way for all voices to be heard in the manner they are comfortable, but more importantly you invite ideas and shared ownership so that your team understands that they can make an impact and create change for the better, no matter their position in the organization.

7 INCENTIVIZE GOOD WORK

As one year was ending and another was about to begin, my hotel at that time, had somehow slipped to a #2 ranking in our comp set on TripAdvisor. In a seasonal beachfront location where we owned the majority of the market share, it was not where we should be ranked and not how we envisioned ending the year or starting another. I knew that a motivational email or communicating in huddle to be better together wasn't going to be enough to get us over the hump. It was going to require me to be more creative and raise the stakes a bit. That's when I decided that I would put myself on the other side of a wager, one I hoped would be enough to incentivize my team to get more positive reviews and get us back at #1. But if they succeeded, it was going to cost me. Not in terms of money, but rather warmth and well being. That's because I agreed to jump in the ocean if our team was able to get us back to #1 within 30 days. Now you're probably thinking jumping in the ocean is actually quite refreshing, especially if it's a hot summer day. But you got to remember that wasn't the case here. It was December, so there was snow on the ground, and the water...well it wasn't as refreshing as it was frigid. It was one of those risk vs reward scenarios that I knew people would buy into. I mean come on, who wouldn't want to watch and film their boss jump into the icy ocean. So, I started by sending a message out to all employees with a picture of me by the ocean, telling them what our goal was and what was at stake. That was on December 15th. After that, I just continually promoted and hyped it up each and every day whether it was at huddle, in meetings, or in passing with employees in the back hallway.

It was important that the team knew that their individual contributions could make an impact and in this particular case would benefit the business, and get me, their boss, diving into ice water. Little did I know how quickly they would be inspired into action. The team really rallied around the idea and collectively made a sincere effort to elevate our service level on day one. Review ratings began growing instantly, improving our chances to regain our top spot.

On January 4th, just a few days into the new year, we actually made it happen and accomplished our hard fought goal. We had regained our dominant position as #1 on Tripadvisor. It was time for me to bite the bullet, and so I agreed to jump in the ocean just two days later. In only 20 short days, my team accomplished our goal through hard work and discipline. Around 20 people joined me on that cold day to watch as I delivered on my promise. As I ran towards the water fully clothed, everyone pulled out their phones and cheered as I dove into the freezing cold water.

Many were surprised I actually went through with it. The moment my body was submerged I immediately lost my breath, and my body went into shock. I jumped out from under the water and gasped for air, wondering why in the world I agreed to this. As I quickly ran out of the water, grabbed a towel and began walking back to a warm car I stopped, and I took a moment to appreciate the effort that got us here.

Because of our shared ownership and an opportunity for everyone on our team to make an impact on the outcome, it inspired action that led us to accomplish great things. Later that day, we had a scheduled all employee town hall meeting, where we shared the clip filmed earlier that showed me delivering on my polar bear plunge promise. We then celebrated with confetti, an accomplishment that helped open my team's eyes to the potential we had when we had a common goal and collective responsibility. Incentivizing good work in this way becomes contagious; it gets people talking and joining efforts to be part of something bigger than themselves. But it's just as important to incentivize and reward individual efforts and results as well.

I've talked about how we are conditioned at a very young age to seek approval and recognition. With that knowledge you should continue to reward the behaviors you want to see from your team. Just like me incentivizing my team to get back to #1 by being willing to jump in the icy ocean, you too, can create employee driven initiatives that elevate their output individually and collectively. In this chapter I will provide you a workable set of initiatives that will not only motivate your employees day-to-day, but also produce elevated effort levels weekly, monthly, quarterly and beyond. Consistency is key, so setting the standard and incentivizing over time will develop a more sustainable growth pattern. Let's get into it by starting with a rather traditional option that is not followed through on as much as you would think.

Employee of the Month

In my experience I have seen Employee of the Month done a number of negative ways. Whether it's inconsistent month to month, chosen based on favorites, decided based on equal distribution of the award, or worse, not at all, they're all equally bad. They will have the opposite outcome you're aiming to produce. Many companies will have a standard in place but won't follow through on it. But it's important you don't make those same mistakes. That's why I always say consistency is the key to a successful culture. What you need is a framework that is strategically designed to incentivize your employees for what you value most effort, attitude, energy, and results. More specifically you want to incentivize those who go above and beyond for each other and your guests. In order to know someone went above and beyond you need to seek others doing good. So my version of Employee of the Month is just as much about the winner as it is about the journey. You need to promote others to seek the good and share their stories.

Sharing stories is a powerful thing. People don't want to be told what to do, they want to feel compelled to do it through inspiration. This is the power of storytelling. When people can identify with someone else in a story they are more willing to adopt those same behaviors and attitudes. So if your employees are constantly sharing stories about their co-workers who they've noticed have been going above and beyond, it has 2 immediate effects. The first is, it encourages everyone to start looking for the good and find people to celebrate rather than exploit. The second effect is relatability. Your people will identify with those in the story and will want to be mentioned as well, changing their effort level to do so. These effects will be positively contagious and elevate everyone's energy and effort which will result in elevated outcomes. You start by sharing stories in huddle and extend it into your departmental meetings, and over time, more and more people will come prepared with celebration stories about one another.

With that said, the nomination process for Employee of the Month is just that, sharing stories. So you create a nomination form with 2 nomination slots. Employees are then encouraged to provide examples, observations, or stories of a specific team member, based on their interactions and contact with that employee. These stories should highlight examples of where and how the employee went above and beyond for a co-worker or guest over the last 30 days and why they are deserving of Employee of the Month honors. By making the sharing of stories a daily occurrence, it keeps people focused on finding people doing good, remembering how, and sharing to encourage others to do the same daily. Over time, this allows the nomination and selection of a winner to become simplified. This process also removes that frustrating end of month frenzy where everyone is in a mad dash to nominate who they can think of in the moment, that often results in someone winning who may not have actually deserved it. By keeping it consistent, you will start seeing extra effort and recognition for it every single day.

Now that we are consistent in elevating effort and celebrating it daily, you might be asking yourself what gifts should the winner be rewarded with? The gifts I typically reward to the winner are $100 cash, a parking pass for 30 days when applicable, and getting their picture taken to be celebrated via email with a write up, then the picture is posted in the breakroom for the next 30 days. The importance of the write up is to explain why they won. This is important because it provides a roadmap to those striving to be recognized next. It sets expectations as well as upholds the integrity of the program. Oh, did I mention this initiative is also employee nominated, meaning all the stories of people doing good are peer to peer. This eliminates any negative connotation or belief that it involves favoritism, increasing engagement and trust from the moment you start and every step of the way after.

More important than any gift provided, is the unexpected and life changing way we celebrate our winners of Employee of the Month. Have you ever heard the quote, "Praise in public, correct in private"? This is great advice. I double down on the praise in public part in how we celebrate. Let me explain what I mean. You start by inviting everyone working that day to what is called prize patrol. You will obviously need to orchestrate this part at a time and day when the winner is working. Prize patrol consists of tambereens and a portable speaker which you will use to play a dance song of your choosing. Prize Patrol is a celebration not limited to the winner and their manager, it is open to all employees to join.

Some employees will join the parade and others will patiently wait in the lobby for your arrival. When everyone has arrived for prize patrol, you turn on the tunes and begin giving out confetti to each person in attendance. Once everyone is armed and ready to dance, you turn up the volume and begin to march together towards your lobby where the winner and many others are patiently waiting to celebrate. If you are trying to visualize what this may look like, picture something similar to how chain restaurants usher their singing waiters out to the floor in order to collectively sing happy birthday to an embarrassed kid. In our case everyone knows we are celebrating someone, they just don't know who.

In the lobby is a member of HR who has the confetti cannon locked and loaded, and has formed a circle of employees. As the prize patrol enters the lobby area, the group waiting begins to clap as both groups form together into one big circle. You then jump in the middle chanting and getting the group excited in anticipation to find out who the winner is. In your back pocket sits a thank you note with the winners name on it, filled with $100 cash and a parking pass. As you look around the room clapping to the beat and attempt to spot the winner's location in the circle, you notice all the smiling faces and positive energy exuding from those that surround you. That's when you stop and say, "Please join me in celebrating our Employee of the Month...pause...pause...BRIAN!" As you call out his name, the confetti cannon is initiated and begins showering everyone in the lobby. You simultaneously bring him to the middle of the circle and everyone around him throws confetti at him in celebration. He's in shock and disbelief, yet so very happy and smiling ear to ear. He's overwhelmed with joy out of appreciation for the recognition. The whole group claps collectively in celebration of his accomplishment. You then capture the moment in a group photo with Brian front and center. It's also important to get a photo with their direct supervisor which will be sent to them, as well as posted in the breakroom in recognition of this month's winner. Yes, they got a $100 and a parking pass but this moment means so much more. They are recognized and rewarded in public surrounded by those they work hard with and care about in a way a rare few ever get a chance to experience. As the celebration concludes, the winner may not want this special moment to be over, and so they decide to make confetti angels on the floor as people begin cleaning up. Others may be overwhelmed with emotion and need to sneak away to the bathroom to regroup because frankly no one has ever cared or shown appreciation in that way before. Regardless of the reaction, the outcome of this approach will deliver results that positively impact the life of your people. That kind of impact is what we all need to be more deliberate in delivering.

Manager of the Quarter

Many companies will have an employee of the month program but will forget to recognize their leaders unless they hit their numbers. Your managers are the ones equipping and coaching your employees. They are the ones providing a roadmap for employees to achieve their goals. They are also the ones leading departments to operational and financial success. So it's crucial we keep them motivated and not neglected. Many times when we speak on improving employee experience, it's strictly in regards to line level staff. We work with the leadership teams to develop plans to improve line level employee experience but so often there's no incentive for managers to exceed expectations themselves. The thinking is that managers make a good salary so why do they need to be incentivized any further to do the job they are paid to do. But that's just the wrong way of thinking. That's why I recommend implementing a Manager of the Quarter Program.

The way this is set up is very similar to Employee of the Month. However unlike EOM it is graded monthly and celebrated quarterly. The reward is $300, and it's celebrated in the same way as previously described, just in your quarterly town hall with all employees present which heightens the excitement and celebration. Similarly, it is employee nominated. This is because if you are really trying to get to know someone's leadership style and ability you should ask their people if they are delivering, not who they report to. The leadership review form is provided in a bingo style form that allows employees to grade their manager on 25 different deliverables necessary to be considered a great leader. They are graded on things like whether they provided ownership opportunity, heard their team's ideas, showed genuine appreciation, etc. Only if their manager hits the necessary percentage of 85% or above on their deliverables can they even be considered for nomination. This again is done each month within each quarter, meaning they need to be consistent. At the end of the quarter, if they are hitting the mark, their name is part of the nomination ballot. Employees then pick the particular leader they believe deserves the honor by providing a story backing up their belief. This tool is also a measuring stick for leaders to hold themselves accountable month to month to ensure they are doing their part to lead, care, and support their team to the best of their ability. Please see below for what this sheet looks like and what's included to be considered for your own implementation.

Involved in Team Building	Had a one on one with my Manager	Enjoyed a Team Outing	Received a Thank you note from my Manager	Involved in additional Training
Perfect attendance celebrated	We celebrate my personal wins	My Manager supported in a time of need	My suggestions were acted on	I was shown genuine appreciation
I feel involved in Department al decisions	My wellness is encouraged	confetti culture	My work/life balance is encouraged	Resources are supplied when needed to do my job
I am provided ownership opportunities	Encouraged to get involved in the community	Shown a road map for achieving my goals	Incentivized for good work	Im involved in solving problems
My ideas are heard	I am empowered	I am supported	I was provided feedback on my performance	I am encouraged to collaborate

This sheet was developed through research and experience and really creates a clear roadmap for sustainable success in a leadership role. You may ask yourself; am I even able to hit all these in a given month? The answer is yes. The only reason you may not hit them all is because one or more may not apply to a given role or relationship. When you have a framework designed and implemented to have these 25 things be the rule not the exception, that's when things begin to change for the better. This list is then no longer daunting or overbearing, it's a way of life. We make time and have time for the things that matter. So it's time to make sure your managers feel they matter. By creating a quarterly incentive for managers to be recognized, you will not only boost contributions and impact, you will also provide another opportunity to celebrate and cheer each other on.

Employee & Manager of the Year

The way that Employee & Manager of the Year nominations are selected is slightly different than the monthly and quarterly awards. In that, those up for the larger annual awards had to have won monthly or quarterly to be on the ballot. The 12 Employee of the Month winners throughout the year will be the only employees available for selection when voting for Employee of the Year. Same goes for the Manager of the Year. The 4 winners of Manager of the Quarter are the only ones eligible to be selected as Manager of the Year. Otherwise, it devalues the purpose of the monthly and quarterly awards, and removes any motivation for people to exceed expectations consistently. There needs to be structure in this process otherwise it becomes a popularity contest at the end of the year, and people start campaigning to get votes from their colleagues. That devalues the award and the honor received in winning it. So keep it simple and smart and design a structure that has no holes in it. That way, this process only adds value to your organization and its people rather than dividing it. Those nominated from the list still need a story backing up why they believe this individual deserves the award. If the nomination form consists of just a name, the vote does not count.

Winning these prestigious awards is a very big deal and so it's very important you make it feel special. Spare no expense when designing your trophies. Make it something so special that they take it from job to job just to keep it in eyesight in celebration of their achievements.

On the night of the celebration of these awards (your annual employee party), it's important to recognize not just the winners, but those who were nominated as well. I recommend sharing the nice things said about them in a montage of photos and write ups on a wall near the entry of the event to be noticed and read when entering. When recognizing the winners later in the night, I think it's better you bring those up on stage who voted and supported them, allowing them to say it in person. Unfortunately, it's just so rare anymore for people to say really nice things about you prior to moving on to a new job, or worse yet, leaving this earth, so make this a priority in your organization to recognize people and the value they add. Use that moment as anticipation rises, to get the emotional juices flowing in the room by inviting their Manager and the employees who voted for her to set the stage by providing stories of why she's so deserving.

To be appreciated by her peers and her superior, all in one moment, makes for a very significant and overwhelming experience that she won't soon forget. Once the sharing has concluded, you add to the anticipation and excitement of hearing her name called with a drum roll. As her name is announced and she walks towards the stage, the confetti cannons shoot off, showering the room with positive energy and excitement for her accomplishment. At this moment she feels like she just won a league MVP award, and she'll share a speech about all those who helped her along the way as long as she can muster up the words and keep it together emotionally. Moments like this change someone's life. It's a memory of recognition and reward that will never be forgotten, and will shape the way she and others view her in the weeks and years to come. Be intentional. Don't take this opportunity for granted, and be sure to design your celebration in a way that you believe creates the greatest impact for your team.

You would then apply the same structure in announcing the Manager of the Year. Build them up through shared story and appreciation and delivering a slam bam confetti finish that celebrates them and their moment, while simultaneously inspiring and igniting the fire in so many others watching to want to strive for the same the following year. This is their shining moment, but it's also yours. This moment shows everyone in that room your company values its people, and that you put people above protocol and more importantly above profit.

Nomination Celebration

Something I learned, may have greater value than actually winning any of these awards, is finding out you were nominated. As strange as that may sound, it's true. The reason for that is because roughly only 8% or less of your employees will actually win Employee of the Month, but the number of nominations is significantly higher. As previously stated, we rarely share enough about how much we love and appreciate people, and if we do we wait until it's too late. So if you have the ability to create a nomination hallway or wall, it may be one of the single best decisions you've made as a leader. So many companies miss this opportunity, because they don't realize it's value from the employee's perspective.

I will never forget what was said when I first introduced a nomination hallway. At that hotel, we had the ability to line our whole back hallway with snap frames and posters, displaying those who were nominated with nice stories written about them. Once the hallway was designed and the posters were up and confetti was drawn all over the walls, I decided to mention it in huddle and invited the group into the hallway to see it. At this moment I just stood there and observed and listened. As they walked down the hallway to see and read what was said about their peers, one of the employees was surprised to find herself nominated. She was very outspoken so she said out loud, "It's just really nice to know I'm nominated and that I'm recognized by my peers. We have never been made aware who was nominated in the past, just the winners, so this is really nice." That's when I realized not only the value of the nomination itself, but more importantly the value of the recognition and stories written by their peers. This was another public display of appreciation that made a significant and immediate impact. After snap frames are purchased, this hallway is easy to maintain and has no additional cost, but the initial investment reaps great returns. It keeps people motivated and inspired, and constantly walking through in hopes to find their photo and read what was written about them. What's also interesting is whether they win or not, they ask to have the poster to either take it home, to put it in their lockers, or post them in their department areas in celebration. These little things all add up to a big deal and that's the power of incentivizing. With the nomination hallway, it's not about the reward but the recognition. Remember, as kids we are conditioned to need and seek recognition and reward, so finding that balance is crucial to your cultural success.

An additional way I recommend recognizing and promoting those nominated for employee of the month is hosting an "All In" breakfast or luncheon prior to the winner being celebrated. What this "All-In" event does is remove the I-never-win attitude that will deflate motivation, and instead promotes an All-In attitude for what it takes to be great.

Remember, as a leader, like a parent, you want to encourage and nurture the behaviors you want to continue to see. So, If you want those who were nominated to continue the behavior and effort that got them there, you need to still recognize them, involve them, and engage them in celebration for their efforts because only one will win. Winning isn't everything. Sometimes people just want to be part of something, so by hosting a luncheon where you recognize all the individuals who were nominated, you promote and inspire more of that same behavior.

At the All-In event, you would take a moment to speak on the amazing effort exhibited by each of them and express your sincerest gratitude for their extra effort over the last 30 days. You would then share the stories written about them on their nomination forms helping them realize they matter, people around them care, and that they are noticed by their peers for their contributions. During the luncheon, you would celebrate those nominated, while creating anticipation and excitement as you get closer to celebrating the winner. The luncheon would be hosted and orchestrated on the day in which the winner was working, so that there wouldn't be an issue with them not attending. From the lunch, you would directly lead into prize patrol as previously described which would start the celebration process. By hosting this lunch, you not only celebrate the positive behavior and the individuals exhibiting it, but you also inspire more of it. You promote celebrating others, win or lose, while creating friendly competition and motivation to want to be crowned the winner.

We want everyone nominated to feel they have a chance to win, but not necessarily need to win. We want each person to be motivated to bring more people to the table, as well as stay there themselves. That's why you provide an award at the end of the year to any person who is nominated every month following their first nomination. Because it's more about each person continuing the positive behavior and contagiously inspiring others to do more of the same. The hope is that each month, more and more people are nominated and added to the All-In club. Over time, people begin to buy-in to the All-in attitude. Not because you tell them to, but because they are inspired to. That will have a profound impact on your operation, your guest experience, and the way your company makes them feel.

Promotion Recognition

Remember to keep perspective and appreciate the power of moments. The advancement of an employee from their current position to a higher one is a peak life moment. It gives them new responsibility and authority and will change their life in more ways than one, including financially. To move up in an organization creates great pride in oneself, and so it's important to consistently recognize those individuals who achieve their goals.

Promotions also increase employee satisfaction and productivity. When employees believe they have an opportunity to be promoted they are much more likely to be satisfied, productive, and remain with the company which improves retention. Reverting back to what I said earlier about storytelling, and the impact of relating to a character or in this case a colleague, you need to remember that seeing a coworker being promoted helps someone else believe it's possible for them. Increasing their belief increases their effort and energy levels. Believe to achieve as they say. So that's why it's important you publicly recognize promotions in a letter by the time clock and in your monthly newsletter.

I still have a copy of all the letters or emails of promotions I've received over the years. Kind words written about you recognizing your hard work and dedication go a long way. Sometimes it's nice to pull them up and reflect on how far I've come and reassure and reaffirm my belief in my abilities. I am sure you can agree that's something we all need every once in a while. If you know the impact that has on you, you need to know it's the same for others, as well. That's why I encourage you to implement this practice of recognizing promotions into your culture so that it's another added element of positive impact for those involved and beyond. Below you can find a sample letter

I've sent in the past that helps you understand what should be included when putting yours together.

Hi Team,

We are excited to announce the promotion of [insert name] to Front Desk Supervisor at [insert company]. She started last March while still attending the Institute of Amazing Education with a focus on Hotel and Hospitality Management, where she graduated in August with the Legendary Leadership Award. Since her start she has gone great lengths to provide both our internal and external guests with memorable experiences, while constantly looking to absorb more knowledge to propel her growth and opportunity. [insert name] is very passionate about our guests and their experience and we have no doubt she will have great success in her new role. A promotion such as this makes me so very proud and I am sure you will all join me in congratulating and supporting [insert name] in her new role. I am excited for what the future holds and I believe this is another great step forward in continuing our most successful year yet!

Taking the time to write these kind words and including their personal wins and the value added to the organization by promoting them makes all the difference in the world. Again it gets the person promoted to feel pride, and inspires the people reading it to be the next one on the list.

In Conclusion

In this chapter I have provided you with multiple ways to reward the behaviors you want to see from your team.

Incentivizing comes in many forms and is done through recognition and reward. It's a motivator and an encouragement that we are all conditioned at an early age to seek out. Whether it's incentivizing employees to get you back to #1, striving to be the best leader or employee possible, or having an All-In attitude, through recognition and reward you can boost contribution and impact for the better. My hope is that from this chapter, you are inspired to create your own employee driven initiatives. Your new ideas once implemented will ensure consistent energy and effort in your hotel or organization, and help your team develop a more sustainable growth pattern impacting your people, processes, and profits year over year.

8 PERFORMANCE FEEDBACK & COACHING

High performing employees often leave a company due to frustration with, and lack of support from, their direct supervisor. Reasons can range from lack of communication, resources, advancement opportunity, trust, praise, or all the above. Unfortunately, that last one has been true for me in recent history. I recently had a boss who was an emotionally driven manager who ruled with fear not fairness. He would constantly fly off the handle and so the team was forced to walk on eggshells around him. Not knowing what kind of mood he would be in created an unpredictable work environment. Great cultures are built on the foundation of consistency, so his unpredictable behavior created an inconsistent culture of uncertainty and favoritism for those who catered to his needs. He lost my respect, and we lost many great people because of him, yet he was never held accountable or provided coaching to be better from it. Why? Because he was expected to know what he was doing in a role of his caliber. This lack of coaching or accountability is uncomfortably common across all industries, yet companies refrain from taking action to change it. Many times, people get promoted into managerial roles because they are great contributors and results driven but don't have the slightest clue how to lead others to do the same. They then develop bad habits, continue to climb the ladder, and do damage to many along the way.

In order to resolve this, there needs to be ongoing daily situational coaching at a micro level as well as mandatory monthly leadership labs that continue the practice and development of your leaders and their skillset on a macro level. Look, I get it. Your first thought is, who has time for that? But the consequences for lack of action in this case can be detrimental to your people and your business. When a manager isn't intentionally taught to be a leader it leaves them to their own devices, developing bad habits with no guidance or understanding of how they affect people, productivity, processes, and ultimately your profits. When a manager becomes power hungry, barks orders, and sets unrealistic expectations it's contagious. It will then be adopted by many and make negative the norm. That's why it's so important to stay connected with your direct reports so that you can continue to coach them through constructive yet motivational feedback daily.

Performance feedback is proven to boost motivation and morale. It helps people know where they stand and holds them accountable to build from where they are to where they could be. It keeps the focus looking forward and rewards your top performers. Creating this structure only creates benefits for your culture and company. The problem is, most managers tend to not be equipped or prepared to deliver feedback or be good managers in the first place. You promote a doer and expect them to be a delegator. You promote a high performer in order to duplicate their efforts across their team, but provide no support or guidance because they are a manager and they should now know what they're doing. It's a failing system. It fails your leaders, their teams, and your organization. So it's time to make a change.

Leadership Coaching

Leadership is not a position you take, it's a decision you make. Yet so many assume that once a person has a manager title they are automatically prepared and outfitted with the experience and training needed to lead a team. That thinking can't be further from the truth. It is so very rare that a manager is coached prior to being thrown to the wolves. Accountability starts with the leader of a team, therefore it's 100% your responsibility to properly equip your management team with the time, tools, and training to be at their best and deliver their best daily. Otherwise, you leave room for uncertainty and unpredictability which delivers turnover and under performing employees.

Coaching is a vital tool that creates on-going development of the skills required to be great leaders. That's why I suggest you implement a monthly mandatory 12 course Leadership Development curriculum that reviews the important elements of being a great leader, one month at a time. Break down best practices and deliver practical exercises to help them learn it and apply it in their day to day operation. By reviewing things like communication, expectations, how to conduct a meeting, and people development, you can then shape your managers into the leaders you hope they will be. Otherwise, you leave it up to chance, and allow their lack of leadership to force good people out unknowingly.

Monthly leadership coaching is a great start but it doesn't stop there. One-on-one in the moment daily situational teaching is vital to your success as well. You have to remember that even a professional athlete practices everyday. They don't just get drafted and hit cruise control riding on the coattails of their past selves. They work hard and practice every single day to improve. Why? Because practice provides poise, and we all have an urge to want to be better.

Only with practice can you be ready to face the unexpected and create a positive outcome. The point of training is to actually get to a place where you don't need to think about what to do next. It helps you to react wisely, rather than blindly. When confronted with a challenge you can then remain even keeled and act from clarity, which can't be learned in the moment.

In addition to daily coaching and monthly leadership training, I also highly recommend what's called the 5Ps Proactive Plan. You may remember briefly hearing about this in a previous chapter but I believe it is important to reiterate and explain further its positive impact.

Proactive people are constantly moving forward, looking to the future, and making things happen. They're actively engaged, not passively observing. Being proactive is a way of thinking and acting. The purpose of this 5 step system is to help you as a manager or supervisor to identify the top issues or problems that are occurring within your department and what you can do to fix them in advance before they become detrimental to your department and the operation.

The reason I first implemented this tool was because where I was working at the time was constantly putting people on PIPs, or Performance Improvement Plans. The purpose of a PIP was to define serious areas of concern, gaps in work performance, reiterate expectations, and allow the opportunity to demonstrate improvement and commitment. This document was a last resort on a larger systemic problem. The real issue was that our managers were not trained, so they did not value the concept of ongoing training with their teams. They spent more time putting out fires then preventing them. We were very reactive, and we needed to change. Simply put, either you run the day or the day runs you. So we introduced the 5ps Proactive Plan to become more intentional in our approach. The 5Ps Proactive Plan was broken out into 5 sections including predict, prevent, plan, participate, and perform. My favorite section is participating because as a leader you need to take an active role in developing your people. Below you will find how it is broken down so that you too can utilize this concept in your organization.

> **Step 1 - Predict:** *What are the top 5 issues in your department that you foresee being a problem that your employees deal with on a daily basis?*
> **Step 2 - Prevent**: *What are ways you can prevent these 5 situations from happening?*
> **Step 3 - Plan**: *Plan Ahead! What tools or resources can you*

use to help?

Step 4 - Participate: *What are some ways you can get involved with your employees to help them fix each problem you listed in your department?*

Step 5 - Perform: *Set dates and goals for yourself to perform on these resolutions for each issue! SMART- Your goals should be specific, measurable, attainable, relatable and time based.*

This tool is utilized at a leadership level but directly impacts your line level counterparts. Once this was implemented at my property, with time and discipline, we began to change our habits for the better. We became more intentional and more impactful, shifting our mindset from "last resort" to "let's support". For this reason, I encourage you to add something similar to your leader's tool belt.

Everything mentioned above is also directly applicable to your departments line level employees. There should be coaching and monthly training for them too. Don't wait and only train people at your monthly meetings. It needs to happen consistently. Strategically plan out your training sessions for those who need it and identify when they need it by using your 5Ps Proactive Plan. This will allow you to get ahead of problems, engage with your staff, and empower them to not only make decisions but be confident in making the right ones.

Coaching starts the moment the onboarding process starts. It's not enough to just give an employee a stack of SOPs, review them, and have them shadow for a week with an unmotivated employee, yet this is the norm in the onboarding process for most companies. Your employees will not retain the information this way or be able to apply it. Inadequately trained employees are then likely to experience poor job performance and increased levels of work-related stress, especially if it's never reviewed and practiced with supervisor support again. To truly understand the value that training adds to your organization, it can help to look at how the lack of training affects it. By not training your employees you can negatively affect their productivity, safety, efficiency, confidence, and retention. Training is imperative in running a successful organization, so I hope this chapter motivates you to make the proper adjustments in better equipping your people.

Bi-Annual Evaluations

I swear everywhere I've been hired in my career, across multiple industries, someone comes to me in the first week of being there and tells me they haven't had a review in 3 years. Talk about a demotivator. From the employee perspective, what's the point of even trying at that point. If people aren't getting even a simple annual review they sure as hell aren't getting recognition or reward from anybody. Many times, the response I get from those who don't conduct employee performance evaluations is, "we were just so busy it got away from us," or, "revenues were down this year we couldn't afford it," or, "we changed over management and it fell through the cracks." Regardless of the excuse, it's unacceptable. Don't allow your organization or your people to make a habit of making excuses. Instead make a habit of delivering on your promises. Your employees deserve better, and the effect it has on effort ultimately impacts your profitability.

While employee evaluations over the years have become less and less popular, I still value them enough to implement them bi-annually. The reason I continue to use them is it creates fairness, transparency, people development, and a roadmap for achieving goals for all. Yes, performance reviews have costs, but they have benefits, too. I recommend doing one at the start of each year. This initial evaluation has no financial implications but provides each employee an understanding of where they stand and a set of expectations that helps them reach their full potential. That way they have a clear roadmap on how to get the best possible increase come July. The second evaluation is financially incentivized. These evaluations allow you to see the management potential in employees and proactively create a road map that promotes learning before poor performance. Mindsets will shift around the building when getting feedback is seen as an opportunity and not an obstacle. Consistency in how people are financially incentivized is an area of opportunity for many organizations, so I want to be sure to provide my best practices.

Many employee evaluation packets are designed well, with good structure, but do not provide direction on how employees should be financially incentivized. On the back of many evaluations there is a line to reveal the salary increase, which usually does not correspond with the grading scale typically explained on the cover sheet. I know many managers are then unclear on what is an appropriate increase based on this format, which then leads to employees not having consistency in what's expected or delivered. That has a direct impact on budgeting and your bottom line. That is why I advocate for the below percentages to correspond with the typical grading on the cover of your Employee Evaluation:

Level 5: Exceeds Job Requirements = 8% increase

Level 4: Meets and Usually Exceeds Requirements = 6% increase

Level 3: Fully Meets Job Standards = 4% increase

Level 2: Improvement Needed to Meet Job Requirements = 2% increase

Level 1: Does not Meet Job Requirements = No increase

Creating this structure allows you to prepare and build these expectations into each year's budget. This grading scale provides clarity for managers and employees alike, and motivation to strive for more. It keeps you consistent, unbiased, and strictly based on performance. So now that you understand the value in being consistent in your numbers, it's important you learn the value of consistency in your delivery.

Performance evaluations can be viewed as one of the more uncomfortable interactions between supervisors and employees if not done in the proper way, but when conducted professionally, openly and honestly, evaluations can help enhance work relationships and personal performance. By ensuring your team members feel valued and appreciated, and by providing constructive yet motivating on-going feedback your team members response to a performance review will be dramatically better than if you don't. They will have an open mind and see it as a learning opportunity if improvement is needed and discussed. Coming from a supportive angle, not a place of blame, is key. It should be a 2-way conversation on how you can help each other improve, not a transaction where you talk at them and give them an ultimatum. You need to provide them a voice. Find out their goals, create a roadmap, and discuss ways you can support them along the way. Only make promises you can keep. Dangling a carrot leads to disappointment and departure. Trust me I've seen it first hand. Honesty is really the most important thing. Be transparent, be direct, and communicate expectations. It's important you go out of your way to boost their self esteem and help them believe in themselves. That way they leave the room with confidence and understanding regardless of the outcome.

In Conclusion

After reading this chapter you now have a better understanding of what's needed to create sustainable individual and team success through ongoing coaching and performance review. The positive impact of these ongoing efforts builds confidence, productivity, morale, support, and profitability if consistent. The bottom line is, invest time and money in your people and the return on investment will directly impact your bottom line. Write that down!

9 EMPLOYEE ENGAGEMENT

Employee engagement is about developing a relationship between your employees and the organization. You need to engage with what they do, why they do it, and how it impacts the bigger picture. In order for your employees to care about your guests enough to build relationships that build loyalty to your organization, you must first care about *them*. It's all about relationships and care. Caring for people on your team is a real differentiator between success and failure as a leader. That's why it's so important in the hotel industry to shift our focus from the guest and their experience, to those who provide it.

In the early parts of my career, I was under the impression that you should keep your distance from your team outside the walls of your organization. I was taught that getting too close had consequences. You should show interest in them but not jeopardize the operation by developing a close relationship. If you become friends it creates blurred lines and a higher level of difficulty when needing to make tough decisions. I was taught if you care too much you will just get hurt. They will lose respect for you, become disengaged, and unmotivated to listen and follow through, not to mention the effect it would have from the outside looking in. It would create favoritism, and resentment in the eyes of their co-workers. These consequences felt valid to me so I kept my distance. I later realized that approach was the wrong way to go. I wouldn't be able to achieve the level of trust needed to build a successful team if I was keeping my distance. Building trust through care is what families do, so my mindset had to change in order to be better together. That's when I realized I needed to adopt a father-like mindset that allowed me to engage, enable, and empower my people to be better than ever.

In this chapter I am going to reiterate the importance of actively being part of your people's development by staying engaged with them daily. Treat them more like family then employees, and intentionally create a structure and culture that builds and nurtures relationships both at work and beyond. My hope is that by teaching you what not to do, through my learned mistakes, I can help create a path that's easier for anyone who follows behind me.

Commitment to Caring

Parenting is the process of promoting and supporting the physical, emotional, social, and intellectual development of a child from infancy to adulthood. Parenting refers to the intricacies of raising a child. The same concepts apply to leadership. Leadership is the process of influencing or guiding other individuals or teams to reaching their full potential through coaching and development. Leadership refers to the intricacies of raising people up and elevating their abilities. The reason I share this comparison with you is so that you understand in order to be a GREAT leader you must mesh these two together. As a leader, you must care about your people.

Whoever your parental figures were, they cared for you deeply. They nurtured you and picked you up when you were down, building you back up and encouraging your growth and development. They attended your school plays, track meets, chorus concerts, and graduation, supporting your interests through every faze and trend. They were physically, mentally, and emotionally invested in you regardless of whether they liked the same things or not. Why? Simply put, they cared.

The same applies with your team. Remember, we are all conditioned to need to be cared for. It's in human nature. Therefore, as a leader of a team, it is crucial you adopt this same principle and behavior. Like Teddy Roosevelt said, "No one cares how much you know, until they know how much you care." They won't buy into you or your vision if they don't feel you've bought into them first. They need to know that you're invested in their personal and professional interests, growth and development. It's no small task and takes time to nurture, but if you really want to build a connected team you first need to connect with each individual by committing to care.

Walk-a-bouts

Thanking and interacting with employees is the foundation for creating the positive environment you need. So it's important to invest time in connecting with others throughout each day. When you walk by a team member in the hallway or cross by their desk, don't just say, "Hey, how's it going?" and keep walking. Stop for a moment, engage and take the time to hear the answer. It's important you invest your time in getting to know each person better, learn who they are and develop a relationship. Engaging creates engagement. Employees who feel valued make guests feel valued.

Don't make the same mistakes I did as a young leader which was to think my work and my responsibilities were more important than checking on my team. I used to start my workday by making a B-line to my office. I would close the door and avoid getting caught up in conversation or distraction with anyone until I was ready and "available" to do so. I wanted to make sure my schedule and set of responsibilities were the priority, since at the end of the day that's what I was graded on and being held to by my manager. I later learned the hard way through that team's brutal honesty that they felt unsupported, unengaged, and uncared for by my behavior. And they were right.

What I learned over time through many adjustments, was that how good a manager you are is defined not by your direct supervisor, but by the people you lead. If they feel like they're on an island even when you are around, you are failing them miserably. It's this situation and many others after, that helped me shift my mindset and put others first.

When you start your day, check in with your team to see how they are, making sure to thank them for their contributions. Provide opportunity for positive interaction and connection daily. An impactful habit I have learned and developed through failure is walking around for the first and last 30 minutes of my work day, checking in on everyone and high fiving along the way, seeing how they are doing in that very moment, not only as an employee but also on a personal level. I provide support if needed, and an encouraging word when motivation is necessary. This allows them to know and feel that I am physically, mentally, and emotionally invested and available to them just like your parents are for you. Those 5 minutes I spend with each person daily is the most important investment a leader can make. And the reason I started high-fiving along the way is because I've learned the power in transferring positive energy. Energy is contagious so adding a few high-fives into the mix can really help you turn things around for somebody.

Take it from someone who has done the opposite and learned the hard way, this leadershift will truly make a profound impact. It will immediately shift your team's perspective of you and their work at the same time. These simple changes build the foundation for creating the positive environment you need. Over time this will build relationships, and the trust required to be better together.

Before I was married and had kids I was told that you don't realize how selfish you are until you have kids. Being a dad of two girls I totally get that now. All the things you are used to doing at the times you are used to doing them changes. You then have to decide what truly matters and then prioritize accordingly. That's why I don't think I truly understood how to be a great leader until I became a father. That doesn't mean that I became a great leader because I became a father. It just means it changed me for the better. It changed my level of patience, understanding, and empathy. My perspective shifted from me and my needs, to the needs of others, and the people who spent a lot of time around me before and after noticed the difference.

Leadership is about being selfless, not selfish. It's about we, not me. You are not there to be served, but rather there to serve others and it starts with caring for them. Through building caring relationships you can engage, equip, and empower your team members to be at their best and deliver their best daily. Without a doubt they will feel the difference one walk-a-bout at a time.

Skin in the Game

In order to keep your employees engaged, they need to have some skin in the game. They need to be involved in achieving team goals. Keeping your employees involved isnt hard if you know how to do so. Improving employee engagement almost always contributes to improved performance and job satisfaction. Many of the ways to keep your team engaged can be found in the leadership bingo described in Chapter 7. One example is to provide meaning and purpose to what they do by providing insights into how their contributions impact the business and beyond.

The best way to identify a positional purpose is to keep asking why. I like to use a housekeeper position as an example due to the fact that they are typically an undervalued asset to a hotel and known only for cleaning rooms. But it's bigger than that. It's paramount you make sure *they* know it. Let me show you what I mean by simulating a conversation between you and a housekeeper.

You will know you're finished asking questions when you reach the contribution. See below:

Why do you clean hotel rooms?

Because that's what my boss tells me to do.

Why does your boss tell you to?

Because it keeps the rooms from getting dirty and dusty.

Why does that matter?

Because it makes the rooms more sanitary and pleasant.

Why does that matter?

Because it keeps the guests healthy and happy.

BOOM!

Housekeepers don't just clean rooms. Housekeepers are responsible for the health and happiness of the guests. See the difference. It changes everything. When you can help your people shift their perspective and work with purpose, they are engaged. The same thing can be done for any position in any business.

When helping your team better understand why they matter and make a difference, I ask them these same questions in person, to allow them to have the aha moment themselves as they answer. It doesn't stop there. Take it a step further by providing ownership opportunities to your individual team members that helps the collective purpose. Focus on the things that matter. For example, at the Front Desk, the ownership delegated may be inventory, tripadvisor review responses, guest recovery, guest of the day, etc. By delegating these tasks to be owned by others, it helps employees hold themselves and the team accountable by first understanding their impact on the bigger picture. It provides them a clear contribution to the team's goals. This will reinforce their belief as you articulate purpose and create a new vision for the future where they feel included and involved.

Now that they recognized their contributions, it's time to show them their impact by keeping them aware of how the department functions as a whole and needs everyone's dedication to work in unison. It also informs them of the financial implications of their daily actions and how they impact their monthly, quarterly, and yearly goals. I recommend having an area in your department where employees can visually watch their progress in achieving the bigger picture. You may remember, in school, a board to show the tracking of progress. Whether it be a puzzle, a building, or a thermometer, the idea is that it keeps getting built upon at each progression. Creating this type of visual communication peaks people's interest, allowing them to visually watch their impact make a difference in real time while also promoting accountability.

This then leads to a monthly and quarterly financial showing of which departments are delivering or not. Your team wants to know and understand how the business works, what the goals are, and how their efforts in their role in their department impact them, and frankly they need to. They need to understand why decisions are or aren't being made and grasp the gravity of them. The best way to do this is to create a visual in the break room. A simple chart that anyone can understand when reading it.

Don't just post your P&L up there monthly. Your team doesn't need to see intricacies, they just need to see the totals. Simply show how each department measured up against the budget, and how it affects the bottom line today and in the future. Communicating this monthly, and discussing the results in meetings, will keep people engaged and working toward a common goal, collaborating along the way.

Wellness

I started this chapter by discussing the importance of caring. Wellness is a key ingredient to delivering on that promise. Being aware and empathetic to the physical, mental, and emotional wellbeing of your people is more important than ever. Everyone is battling with things unknown, and so it's important you do your part in intentionally and positively impacting your people through wellness initiatives. A great place to start is the offerings you provide to your staff in the breakroom.

What is super interesting about this, is many close minded managers see snacks as an unneeded expense and a potential distraction. I'm here to make sure you know that thought process is wrong. Healthy snack items benefit the business. By leaving your desk you interact with your team more. By providing healthy snack options, you maintain employee energy levels, sustain and enhance productivity, and promote conversation and collaboration. It's like back in school when having snack time kept your engines running well for the remainder of the day. Be strategic in what is provided and be diligent in keeping up on inventory. A great variety of snacks on Monday, but an empty rack from Tuesday until Friday, doesn't do much to sustain effort levels or trust for that matter, so stay on top of this and don't let it be the first thing cut when things don't go your way.

Another way to keep people engaged is creating quarterly Wellness initiatives. The reason I say quarterly is because it's a good place to start. It doesn't force you to over commit and under deliver. If you follow through, try to do this monthly, but quarterly is a great starting point. These initiatives can include group yoga, meditation, spin or bar classes, and even a bike or run club. The idea is to provide them all as options to sign up for, but not make them mandatory. The great thing about introducing such events is not only does it create an outlet for improving wellness, but it also creates opportunity for team unity. These events create common ground and common interest. Bringing people together builds positive interactions and memories that have the power to strengthen your team.

Create Community

Another great way to promote caring within your building, is to show you care in your community. Connecting with your community through volunteering can benefit your team as much as the cause you choose to help. This is why it's super beneficial to dedicate time quarterly to get out there and better your community. Simply put up a voluntary sign up sheet and watch as your team builds bonds that strengthen your business inside and out.

Whether it's painting and prepping a house with Habitat for Humanity, sorting cans at a local fulfillment facility, cooking meals at a local shelter, or marching for change, all of these events bring your team together for a productive purpose. By providing these opportunities, you also help show your team the value in leaving a legacy by helping those who need it. Many of your employees want to make this type of impact but don't know how or where to start. They may even be afraid to venture out alone so by creating these offsite events with relatable members of your work family, you inspire more people to get involved and expand your employees personal and professional impact. That's an amazing thing to be able to do.

It's not enough to just create the events, it's important, as the leader of the group, to be involved, to show up hand-in-hand and work elbow-to-elbow to better the community and the people within it. This again shows your people that you are physically, mentally, and emotionally available to them beyond the four walls of your organization. As a leader it's not just about helping people be better in their position, but more importantly help them be better as people.

A great way to inspire more involvement and promote positive change in the community is to recognize and reward those who not only get involved but *stay* involved. This is why I've created something called Champions of Change. This is an exclusive club whose members have attended all the community events we get involved with whether they are quarterly or monthly in a given year. The idea is to inspire your people to want to better the community, by committing to build a better tomorrow today. Then, you recognize and reward their effort and commitment with a gift at your annual employee party. The long term effect is that people who are initially uninvolved get involved and choose to, based on the opportunity for impact and exclusivity.

In Conclusion

Throughout this chapter I stressed the importance of actively being part of your people's lives by engaging daily. By creating a sustainable structure that involves a commitment to caring, walk-a-bouts daily, purpose and ownership, as well as scheduling wellness and community initiatives, you too can dramatically improve your employee engagement. My hope is that my stories and experiences helped things to click and allow you to not make my same mistakes, while providing a road map for success to anyone who chooses to follow behind me.

10 CONTINUED EDUCATION

As someone who is dedicated to self-improvement and cultivating positive relationships through equipping and mentorship, I make it my mission everywhere I go, to incorporate initiatives that promote continued education. The greatest investment a person can make is in themselves by sharpening their skills through continued education. So often, people will finish going through the school system and cut ties with learning as if it's over. In reality the opportunity to learn, grow, and improve is just getting started.

In school, you're told what to study. Out of school the choice is yours. This is exactly why I have been using every waking minute I have to continue educating myself on leadership and many other topics so that I can better others with the wealth of knowledge I receive by doing so. I'm not the only one. Many people invest in themselves in their free time, and look for it when shopping the market for employment opportunities. Employees simply want an opportunity to learn, and by providing that opportunity, you will retain your people significantly longer. And, it's a misconception that, it needs to cost you a fortune to fulfill this basic need. With 4 simple steps you, too, can check that box to become an exciting and enticing employer option for people who leave to find something better. The four initiatives include departmental workshops, cross departmental training, lunch & learns, and certification reimbursement. Let's start first by discussing how Departmental Workshops not only add value to employees who attend, but also educate colleagues of the intricacies of a department's responsibilities.

Departmental Workshops

Departmental Workshops are designed to serve and enlighten any member of your hotel family who may be interested, yet inexperienced in a department different from their own. They accomplish this by enhancing their knowledge on the processes and procedures that go into a given role through visual and hands on workshops. Involvement in these workshops promotes continuing education, and encourages supporting one another, all while developing stronger cross departmental relationships. It is a positive interaction with only positive outcomes.

Regardless of size, a full-service hotel typically has enough departments and support, that each one can own a month of the year. Departments include but are not limited to Front Desk, Housekeeping, Food & Beverage, Sales, Banquets, Revenue, and Accounting. I have found success with these workshops by having a visual comprehensive breakdown of the department, its responsibility, and it's greater purpose as well as having a hands-on learning component. This accommodates visual, auditory, and kinesthetic learners, allowing you to play to their strengths and learn the best way they know how.

As an example, for a Housekeeping workshop, you may break down a day in the department, reviewing all the essential functions so that people understand the attention to detail, communication, and the hard work required to find success in the day-to-day operation. Then cap it off with an inspection exercise to see if they find all the hidden items, or maybe even a bed making competition. Needless to say, these workshops are not, and should not be, limited to an event space or office area. Teaching in multiple settings ensures engagement and focus, increasing the likelihood those involved leave the workshop retaining the information taught. This same framework can be used to design any department's session. Whether it's making drinks in the Beverage session, or cooking a dish with your Executive Chef in a Food workshop, there are exciting options to create exposure and education for all who are interested.

These paid, one hour monthly departmental workshops, not only educate and strengthen your teams, but they also provide opportunity and exposure for those who may not love the department they were hired in. This allows them a risk-free opportunity to learn more about other areas to help guide them in a new direction. This is an exciting opportunity that shouldn't be taken lightly and allows you to be part of the reason why a member of your team finds their calling.

In addition, we also recognize and reward those who attend all 12 sessions. You should also use attendance as a reference when considering internal candidates for open positions. If there's a position open for a sales coordinator, but when an internal applicant is asked if they attended the workshop for sales and they said, "no" it's going to put their interest and commitment in question. These workshops have a number of benefits and the next initiative takes it a step further.

Walk-a-Mile Program

Next, let's introduce you to the Walk-a-Mile Program. This is the exciting next step from the Departmental Workshops. Similar to the way an internship works, this Bi-annual discovery program allows employees in good standing to trade jobs and explore and experience what it's like to walk-a-mile in the shoes of a colleague. This hands on, paid training in a department and position of their choosing, again is a risk-free opportunity to test out and gain understanding and confidence in the expectation in a role of interest. On the other hand, this program can simply provide additional perspective on how departments work together and the impact each has on the other throughout the day. Regardless of the reason for involvement, its impact inspires new ideas, problem resolution, and mutual respect for coworkers in other roles.

For example, everyone has an underlying presumption that Front Desk Agents just sit around all day and night and get paid more than everyone else to do it. Don't get me wrong, being someone who started in that role, I know first-hand there can be plenty of down time in regards to guest interaction. But there's a lot being done that is unobserved. Any good front office manager keeps his team busy through those times. But from a distance, they ultimately seem to be just standing there browsing the internet. Not until you're locked into a shift at the desk through the Walk-a-Mile program and are responsible for the tasks on that checklist, do you really begin to appreciate the level of competence, patience, communication, and organization it takes to do the job.

Not until you're working the desk and have a line of 10 people at 10am impatiently waiting to check into rooms that of course aren't available (because checkout is at 11am and you were fully committed the night before), do you fully grasp the level of pressure the desk deals with. The level of multi-tasking goes way beyond that. Did I mention the phones were ringing off the hook because today starts a "stay and play" promotion. Oh, and you also have an upset guest at the side of the front desk who refuses to wait in line and insists on speaking to a manager. Since it's early, and no rooms are ready yet, you'll need to take everyone's luggage, but unfortunately your lobby attendant went to the bathroom just before the line arrived so you are now forced to manage all of this on your own. Why? because the mid shift arrives in an hour, your manager just went to talk to that upset guest, and the lobby attendant went on his break without approval, not the bathroom. But the Front Desk just stands around right?

This perspective, regardless of the position one decides to trade into, helps shift any thought that one person or position does more than another. A program like Walk-a-

Mile brings teams together. It provides mutual respect and insights on what it takes to deliver on expectations, the impact these contributions have on the greater goal, as well as continued education and exploration of positions beyond their current commitments. That is why I implement this initiative in partnership with the departmental workshops to provide education and opportunity for all those interested.

Lunch & Learns

Lunch & Learns are voluntary presentations or training sessions that bring people together from across the hotel to collaborate and learn while sharing a much-needed meal. Many times, people in the hotel industry don't even stop to take a break to eat based on the rapid pace of the operational needs, so to create this guaranteed collaborative meal is an attendance motivator. These informal positive interactions also create an atmosphere of personal and team development in an operation that desperately and consistently needs it.

The way to best run a lunch and learn is to be consistent. Consistent in scheduling, in educational delivery, in food quality and quantity, and consistency in internal promotion of the event. I typically schedule these bi-monthly to not over crowd our monthly schedule. The food element is very important, so it shouldn't be the first thing to go just because revenues are down. So, when deciding on the menu, make sure to pick something that doesn't break the bank and can be consistently delivered to your team. The way I structure these events is with the 3 M's. First, we Mingle, then we share a Meal, and then we share our

Message. This allows people to interact and get fed, all in order to be focused on why they are there in the first place; the presentation.

An example of a Lunch & Learn may be a Corporate or Manager Level career path storytelling. I've expressed the value of storytelling countless times in this book. In this case it provides a relatable and confidence building perspective on what other professional journeys look like and could be. It's a platform for your leadership team to explain how they got started, how they ended up where they are, and what important advice they can recommend to those interested in following in their footsteps. Because, if you can provide a path that makes it easier for those coming up behind you, then you are providing tremendous value to your people.

These Lunch & Learn events can be super impactful and continue the education process while inspiring people into action. The variety of topics that can be discussed at these events provides an opportunity to get a wide range of attendees, and like anything, once people start talking about the benefits to their peers, you will continue to build traction as each event passes.

Tuition Reimbursement

A commonly asked for, but rarely delivered on, continued education initiative is College Course Tuition Reimbursement. This is an employee benefit where the employer agrees to pay a set amount for credits towards a degree once complete. While I think this is a great initiative, especially for big companies with deep pockets, I recommend a more refined option that is adoptable by you regardless of the size of your company. That option is certification reimbursement. The reason I recommend this route is because it not only benefits the employee and their future, but it also immediately impacts and benefits your business. Let me explain.

Nowadays there are certifications for just about everything. Whether it's CHRM: Certified hospitality revenue manager, ServeSafe: Food Handler, or CPR, there are industry specific options out there to better your people and your business. Certifications differ from degrees in that their turnaround time is much quicker, and the price is a lot lower, yet surprisingly, the value and impact of the certification can carry greater career value than a degree. Only those serious enough to commit to the process and follow through with flying colors will actually be recognized, rewarded, and reimbursed for their efforts.

This employee benefit has no upfront cost or risk of loss to you. It's about commitment and accountability on the employee's part and if followed through, benefits everyone. Hard to disagree with that. An important element to this initiative is to have employees that are interested first write up their reasoning behind it, the impact it will make on their future and the business, and a commitment to finish the job. Once this is completed it is submitted to HR for approval. If approved, that means both parties agree to the terms which allows the employee to confidently move forward with your support. It's important to note that this commitment is also contingent on their continued employment.

Another crucial part of this incentive is recognizing the

individuals who complete their certification and get awarded reimbursement. Why? Because as I've said many times before, you want to encourage and promote the behaviors you want to see more of. You want your employees inspired and lining up to better themselves, ready to commit to self-improvement. By recognizing those individuals for their effort beyond your 4 walls, it will open the eyes of others to the same opportunity they have, while also showing them that they too can accomplish it. This relatability is powerful stuff and another reason why recognition and reward is an ongoing key to a successful culture.

In Conclusion

By now you understand the importance of providing your employees an opportunity to continually learn, grow, and improve. Now it's time for implementation. Through the discussed initiatives of departmental workshops, the walk-a-mile program, lunch & learns, and tuition reimbursement, you too can build benefits for your people and business alike. You can remove yourself from the negative statistic that affects an employee's longevity at a company and be the reason people not only stay but recruit others to join your team as well. These consistent efforts will be noticed and appreciated by your team members and will be another piece of the puzzle to build your culture's strong foundation.

CONCLUSION

Wow, I just put a lot on your plate, didn't I?! But that's what hard work looks like. It's not supposed to be easy; it's supposed to be worth it. Through implementation of everything we've discussed and consistency from you and your teams, you can be the reason your culture transforms for the better, starting today. It's not going to happen overnight, I can assure you that, but the daily discipline you instill in yourself and your team will be the deciding factor on whether you succeed or fail.

As mentioned, everything rises and falls on the shoulders of a leader, so in order to truly make a difference and change the status quo by putting your people first you need to take ownership of what happens next. You need to encourage and nurture like a parent, while creating structure and tradition similar to a school. The transition similar to a flower being watered will take time to bloom, but it will be the most rewarding and beneficial decision you've ever made.

My hope, as we finish things up, is that you feel the time you've invested in reading this book has added value to you and your teams in some small way. That it inspired new ideas and called you to take action to be the reason things change for the better in your organization.

To my fellow hoteliers reading this book, I hope that you've finally found a book that speaks to you directly and feels relatable and applicable. My goal when writing this book was to create a clear roadmap to achieve your cultural goals that impact your people, process, and profits to not only boost contribution and impact through recognition and reward but more importantly create a home away from home where your employees feel loved, served and cared for like family.

What I've loved about writing my first book is that it's inspired me as I hope it has you. I've been inspired to grow and improve my ideas as I write them. For those who have worked with me in the past, you will notice that some ideas mentioned in this book have matured over time through experience as well as through writing. My hope is that this book will do the same for you; providing you a framework of employee driven initiatives that you too will live, nurture, and continue to grow and improve.

I also hope through reading this book you have begun to appreciate the power of energy and its effect on others. Confetti has become a tool that represents the transforming power of recognition and reward in a company culture. It has the power to immediately transform the energy in any room. As much as confetti is used for that purpose it's even more important and valuable that you learn that same power lives within you too. You can't think showing up and throwing confetti solves all your problems. This is because your cultural transformation starts and ends with you. Being a positive force in your company and teaching others the power of positive thinking becomes a contagious energy that is undeniably seen, felt, and heard by everyone around you. It's a legacy you have the power to create and leave behind everywhere you go just like a trail of confetti. My hope is that you do.

Lightning Source UK Ltd.
Milton Keynes UK
UKHW021048141122
412173UK00012B/2530